TO ORDer BOOKS.

FRIENDS OF ISRAEL G.M.
P.O.Box 908
BELLMAWR, NJ 08031
U.S.A.

THE CHARIOT OF ISRAEL

Exploits of the Prophet Elijah

THE CHARIOT
OF ISRAEL

Exploits of the Prophet Elijah

by
WILL VARNER

THE FRIENDS OF ISRAEL
Gospel Ministry, Inc.
Bellmawr, New Jersey 08031

THE CHARIOT OF ISRAEL
EXPLOITS OF THE PROPHET ELIJAH

Copyright © 1984

The Friends of Israel Gospel Ministry, Inc.
P.O. Box 908
Bellmawr, New Jersey 08031
Cover by Tom Allen
Design and type by Tom Allen Studio

First Edition 1984
Second Printing.............. 1986

Printed in the United States of America
Library of Congress
Catalog Card Number 84-080766
ISBN 0-915540-33-9

DEDICATION

This volume is dedicated to Mrs. Elizabeth Reece,
my grandmother, who, at this writing,
is finishing her "course" (2 Tim. 4:7)
in a nursing home in South Carolina.
Her influence on me has been inestimable.

"The hoary [gray] head is a crown of glory, if it
be found in the way of righteousness"
(Prov. 16:31).

ACKNOWLEDGEMENTS

The student is certainly a debtor to his teachers! Particular thanks must go to Dr. Fred Afman, who first opened to me the riches of the Old Testament writings. Others have written on Elijah before me, and I have profited from all of their writings. I have tried, however, to always have the Hebrew text before me, so I must give thanks also to that brilliant unknown author of 1 and 2 Kings whose inspired account serves as the "text" for these chapters.

Most of these studies were originally delivered as sermons to my former congregation at the Independent Bible Church, Willow Grove, PA. They later appeared in written form in *Israel My Glory,* the publication of The Friends of Israel Gospel Ministry. They were extensively edited and expanded into the present form.

My thanks to Marvin Rosenthal, International Director of The Friends of Israel and honored colleague, whose preaching and example have always been such an inspiration and challenge to my thinking. Many thanks also to my wife, Helen, who has always been a gentle and helpful critic. Thanks also must go to my secretary, Margie Meyer, who labored faithfully in typing and retyping the manuscript.

Finally, I give praise to "the Son of God, who loved me and gave himself for me" (Gal. 2:20).

FOREWORD

You hold in your hand a very special book. At a time in history when literally "of the making of books there is no end," this one is of unique enduring value.

The Chariot of Israel: Exploits of the Prophet Elijah is a special book because of the subject with which it deals. Elijah is one of the stellar personalities of all human history. His life combined frailty and faith in unusual measure. When Elijah was caught up to Heaven, his disciple Elisha cried out, ". . . the chariot of Israel, and its horsemen" (2 Ki. 2:12). It was not, as some suppose, that Elijah was caught up *in a chariot*. Rather, it was his intimate relationship with God which made the prophet "the chariot of Israel." He was a protective hedge about the nation. Had not the prophet single–handedly confronted wicked King Ahab and the four hundred and fifty prophets of Baal?

The Chariot of Israel: Exploits of the Prophet Elijah is a special book because of its unique format. It is impossible to understand Elijah's life and ministry without understanding the physical geography of Israel. Ten special maps have been prepared and appropriately located throughout the text. Their value in helping to understand the truth under consideration is enormous.

The Chariot of Israel: Exploits of the Prophet Elijah is a special book because of its author. I first met Will Varner eleven years ago as we shared the Bible teaching ministry at Lake Erie Bible Conference. On that occasion he shared a series of messages on the life of Elijah. I was so impressed and blessed by the messages that we soon became very close friends. Some years later I invited Will to join The Friends of Israel staff in a leadership capacity. Still later, remembering the blessing his messages on Elijah had brought to my heart, I suggested that he do a series of articles for ISRAEL MY GLORY. Now completely rewritten and expanded, they appear in the book you hold in your hand. Will Varner has unique insight into God's Word, special communicative skills and a hot heart for things eternal. May our Father in Heaven be pleased to breathe upon this labor of love — may it be the first of many volumes to issue forth from his fertile mind — may it ennoble and inform God's people until the day God *catches up* His true Church as He *caught up* Elijah, who, for his hour of history, was ". . . the chariot of Israel . . . ."

Marvin J. Rosenthal

International Director
The Friends of Israel
Gospel Ministry, Inc.

PREFACE

When the word "prophet" is mentioned, the great prophets Isaiah, Jeremiah, and Ezekiel usually come to mind. This is probably due to the fact that these three, along with others like Daniel, Amos, and Malachi, were writing prophets whose books are included in the canonical Scriptures. There were many other prophets, however, who never wrote a book but nevertheless had significant ministries. These nonwriting prophets include such notables as Enoch, Noah, and Abraham (cf. Jude 14; Heb. 11:7; Gen. 20:7). Furthermore, Aaron, Miriam, and Deborah prophesied in some way (Ex. 7:1, 15:20; Jud. 4:4). A partial listing of the nonwriting prophets includes Ahijah (1 Ki. 11), Shemaiah (1 Ki. 12), Jehu and Hanani (1 Ki. 16), and Micaiah (1 Ki. 22). Furthermore, there were prophets whose writings have not been preserved, e.g. Nathan (2 Chr. 9:29), Gad (1 Chr. 29:29), and Shemaiah (2 Chr. 12:15).

But the greatest of all noncanonical prophets was Elijah the Tishbite whose career is described from 1 Kings 17 — 2 Kings 2. Except for Moses, more information is given on his career than any other prophet, even those who wrote long books! Elijah has left his imprint on Jewish tradition. References to him in rabbinic literature abound, and most of these references concern the help that he extends to the poor and the pious. He is associated with numerous traditions as the "forerunner of the Messiah."

To Christians, however, Elijah is equally important. By his Greek name "Elias," he is mentioned no less than twenty-eight times in the Gospels, once by Paul (Rom. 11:2), and once by James (Jas. 5:17). His example of faith and courage has served as a pattern to inspire many a believer to stand up for God and be counted. The author acknowledges that Elijah has always been his "hero" (replacing Mickey Mantle from earlier days!).

The meaning of the prophet's name in Hebrew is "My God is the LORD" (i.e., Jehovah). Elijah let it be known by his name and by his example that the LORD was his God — the only God. May these studies on his life and ministry challenge the modern reader to let it be known that amidst the spiritual idolatry of today, his God is the LORD!

TABLE OF CONTENTS

Dedication v

Acknowledgements vi

Foreword vii

Preface ix

1 ELIJAH: A PERSON LIKE YOU 14
2 LESSONS FROM A BROOK & A WIDOW ... 27
3 OBADIAH: SERVANT OF THE LORD? ... 41
4 THE CONTEST ON CARMEL 54
5 ELIJAH AND THE RAIN 68
6 FROM A MOUNTAIN TO A VALLEY..... 79
7 JUDGMENT IN JEZREEL 92
8 ELIJAH AND AHAZIAH 109
9 ELIJAH'S CORONATION DAY 125
10 ELIJAH'S FUTURE 137

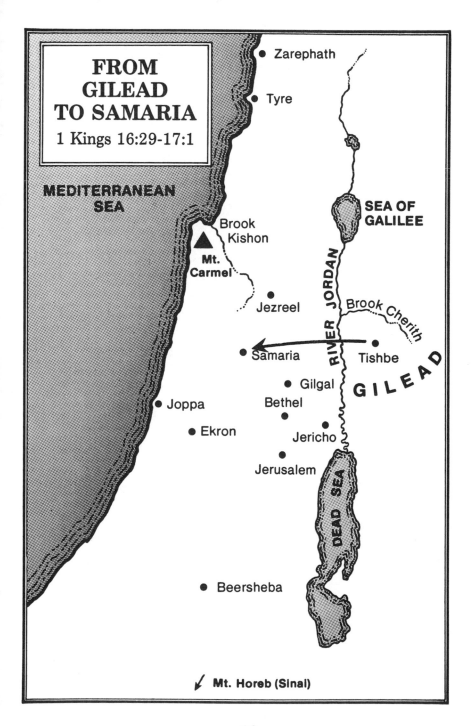

FROM
GILEAD
TO SAMARIA
1 Kings 16:29-17:1

MEDITERRANEAN
SEA

Zarephath

Tyre

SEA OF
GALILEE

Brook
Kishon

Mt.
Carmel

RIVER JORDAN

Jezreel

Brook Cherith

Samaria

Tishbe

GILEAD

Gilgal

Joppa

Bethel

Ekron

Jericho

Jerusalem

DEAD SEA

Beersheba

Mt. Horeb (Sinai)

13

1

1 Kings 16:29–17:1

And in the thirty and eighth year of Asa, king of Judah, began Ahab, the son of Omri, to reign over Israel; and Ahab, the son of Omri, reigned over Israel in Samaria twenty and two years. And Ahab, the son of Omri, did evil in the sight of the Lord above all who were before him. And it came to pass, as if it had been a light thing for him to walk in the sins of Jeroboam, the son of Nebat, that he took as his wife Jezebel, the daughter of Ethbaal, king of the Sidonians, and went and served Baal, and worshiped him. And he reared up an altar for Baal in the house of Baal, which he had built in Samaria. And Ahab made an idol; and Ahab did more to provoke the Lord God of Israel to anger than all the kings of Israel who were before him. In his days did Hiel, the Bethelite, build Jericho; he laid the foundation of it in Abiram, his first-born, and set up the gates of it in his youngest son, Segub, according to the word of the Lord, which he spoke by Joshua, the son of Nun. And Elijah, the Tishbite, who was of the inhabitants of Gilead, said unto Ahab, As the Lord God of Israel liveth, before whom I stand, there shall not be dew nor rain these years, but according to my word.

ELIJAH: A PERSON LIKE YOU

1 Kings 16:29–17:1

We live in a time when people are conscious of sports heroes. There's a Baseball Hall of Fame in Cooperstown, New York, a Football Hall of Fame in Canton, Ohio, and a Basketball Hall of Fame in Springfield, Massachusetts.

God also has a *Hall of Fame*. Hebrews 11 records the membership of what has been called the *Hall of Fame of Faith*. Certain great individuals like Abel, Noah, Abraham and Moses are enshrined there because of the faith which characterized them. They were willing to trust God completely in difficult situations, so He placed them in His *Hall of Fame*.

The prophet Elijah's name does not appear in that chapter, but he is mentioned in a roundabout way. In Hebrews 11:32 we read, "And what shall I more say? For the time would fail me to tell of Gideon, and of Barak, and of Samson, and of Jephthah; of David also, and Samuel, and of **the prophets**." In that word *prophets*, the writer of Hebrews includes all the prophets of the Old Testament, and Elijah was one of those prophets. So Elijah is also enshrined in God's *Hall of Fame*.

There is a saying, "You can lead a horse to water, but you can't make him drink." However, you can give him some salt and make him thirsty. A study of the life of Elijah and the great saints of God in the Old and New Testaments will definitely make one thirsty. As we see how this man trusted God and God used him, it will make us thirsty and inspire us to live like him and to learn lessons from his life that will help us to live for God in this day and age.

The life and ministry of Elijah is recorded in the First and Second books of Kings. This introductory study will consider the subject, "Elijah: A Person Like You."

Elijah comes on the scene very quickly. First Kings 17:1 states simply, "And Elijah, the Tishbite, who was of the inhabitants of Gilead, said unto Ahab, As the Lord God of Israel liveth, before whom I stand, there shall not be dew nor rain these years, but according to my word."

A greater appreciation of this sudden appearance of Elijah on the stage of human history will be gained by examining a few verses at the end of 1 Kings 16.

A Pagan Enthroned

First Kings 16:29–30 records, "And in the thirty and eighth year of Asa, king of Judah, began Ahab [the pagan], the son of Omri, to reign over Israel [where he was enthroned]; and Ahab, the son of Omri, reigned over Israel in Samaria twenty and two years. And Ahab, the son of Omri, did evil in the sight of the Lord above all who were before him."

Now when you stop to think about that statement, you see how amazing it is. Ahab not only did evil; he was worse than all the kings before him! There is a recurring phrase in the books of Kings to describe the wickedness of each king of Israel: "And he did evil in the sight of the Lord, and walked in the way of his father [Jeroboam], and in his sin with which he made Israel to sin" (1 Ki. 15:26, 34; 16:19). Each king of Israel followed in the sinful ways of Jeroboam, the son of Nebat, "who made Israel to sin." You can't find a good one in the whole bunch. Of Omri, the father of Ahab, it is written, "But Omri wrought evil in the eyes of the Lord, and did worse than all who were before him" (1 Ki. 16:25). Omri was worse than all of his predecessors! Omri had a son named Ahab, however, who showed that he was worse than all of the preceding kings including his wicked father. Ahab was, in 20th century terms, *a bad dude*. He was so bad, the Scriptures say that he sold "himself to work wickedness in the sight of the Lord . . ." (1 Ki. 21:25). He was evil incarnate! If the Israelites thought they had something bad with other kings, they really had it bad with Ahab! It was under this king's rule that Elijah appeared. What did Ahab do that was so bad? Look at verse 31: "And it came to pass, as if it had been a light thing for him to walk in the sins of Jeroboam, the son of Nebat, that he took as his wife Jezebel, the daughter of Ethbaal, king of the Sidonians, and went and served Baal, and worshiped him." The former kings were bad, but at least they married other Israelite girls. Ahab, however, looked to his pagan neighbor to the north, Ethbaal, the Phoenician king of the Sidonians who worshiped Baal, the ancient diety whose worship was condemned so strongly by the prophets. Then,

17

in one of those *political* marriages that characterize so much of international relations, he took Jezebel, Ethbaal's daughter, as his wife. When Jezebel brought her beauty into the royal palace of Israel, she brought in her pagan religion as well. "And he reared up an altar for Baal in the house of Baal, which he had built in Samaria" (v. 32). OPEN, UNABASHED IDOLATRY! Under the sponsorship of the king of Israel, a temple to a pagan god was erected in the midst of the capital city! That is the degree to which evil had come to dominate this man. His wife ruled him and was really the power behind the throne. She was doing all that she could to make everyone in Israel worshipers of her god, and she was persecuting those who refused to worship. "And Ahab made an idol; and Ahab did more to provoke the Lord God of Israel to anger than all the kings of Israel who were before him" (v. 33). This is the situation when Elijah comes on the scene — the darkest night of Israel's history.

There is a parallel in the professing *church* of our day. Just as *the world* crept into the worship of Israel, so there are those voices crying out today that the church should be more *worldly* so that we might better relate to the world. Instead of the church going into the world, the world is coming into the church! We do need to relate to the world. But the best way for the church to relate to the world is to maintain its sharp edge so the world can tell the difference between darkness and light. The more the church becomes like the world, the less effect it has on the world (Rom. 12:2; Jas. 4:4).

A Prophecy Fulfilled

Now, notice in verse 34 that during this black hour, a prophecy was fulfilled. Verse 34 states; "In his [i.e., Ahab's] days did Hiel, the Bethelite, build Jericho; he laid the foundation of it in Abiram, his first-born, and set up the gates of it in his youngest son, Segub, according to the word of the Lord, which he spoke by Joshua, the son of Nun."

Upon first reading that verse, you may wonder what in the world it has to do with Ahab and Elijah! What's so bad about a man rebuilding Jericho? Why is this verse included here? After the destruction of Jericho, Joshua pronounced a curse on anyone who would rebuild the city, which is recorded in Joshua 6:26: "At that time Joshua pronounced this solemn oath: Cursed before the Lord is the man who undertakes to rebuild this city, Jericho: At the cost of his firstborn son will he lay its foundations; at the cost of his youngest will he set up its gates" (author's translation). It had now been over 500 years since Jericho's destruction, and the city still lay in ruins. And now during the reign of Ahab, a man said, "I'm going to rebuild Jericho, and I don't care what the curse says!" He rebuilt the city and then the curse fell on his own home. When he laid the foundation of the city, his first son died. He continued to build the city, and finally when he began to construct the city gate, his other son died. The curse was graphically fulfilled. It may have been that this man was so wicked, he actually sacrificed his first son at the foundation, and then sacrificed his second son at the gate. Some commentators hold to that view, although the verse does not

19

clearly state it. Or it may have been some unknown tragedy that occurred — a divine judgment upon his sons. But whatever it was, they died.

This sobering event indicates that it was such a dark night in Israel's history that a man was willing to stand up, mock the Word of God, and declare, "I don't care what God says. I don't care about the curse. I'm going to do what I want to do." That was the mood of the day. He paid for it in the loss of his sons, but he had gone so far that such tragedy didn't really bother him. Although such insensitivity may be hard to comprehend, there are today the same kind of people who willfully, defiantly reject God's authority. When the veneer is removed from the so-called "liberation" movements of our day, that is what is found — a willful rejection of authority — a "do your own thing" attitude. One popular singer expressed this philosophy when he sang, "I did it **my** way." He may have done it his way, but if he didn't do it God's way, he was throwing off God's authority.

It was into this type of situation that God sent His prophet.

A Prophet Unveiled

"And Elijah, the Tishbite, who was of the inhabitants of Gilead, said unto Ahab, As the Lord God of Israel liveth, before whom I stand, there shall not be dew nor rain these years, but according to my word" (1 Ki. 17:1). Out of nowhere, he suddenly appeared on the scene. One commentator said that he who went out of this world in a whirlwind, came in like a tempest.

Let's ponder a couple of truths about this man known as "Elijah the Tishbite." First notice some truths about the **man** and then some truths about **his motives**.

The first thing we want to notice about this man is just that — He was a man. He was *of the inhabitants of Gilead*. Gilead was a region on the east side of the Jordan that was settled during Joshua's days by the tribe of Gad. The region was wild and largely desolate and the residents were mostly rustic farmers and shepherds.

Oftentimes, the great characters of the Bible — the Abrahams and the Elijahs and the Pauls — are considered as *super saints* with halos around their heads to whom most people can't relate. But Elijah was no *super saint* — he was a man. That truth will be graphically illustrated over and over again throughout these studies. He was a man with feelings. As a matter of fact, James 5:17 says it this way: "Elijah was a man subject to like passions as we are . . . ." Or simply stated, one could say, "Elijah was a man just like us . . . ." He had problems. I don't know if he was single or married, but if he was single, he faced the problems of loneliness; if he was married, he faced the problems of providing for a wife and kids. He was a man just like us. And it's good to keep that in mind at the beginning of this series of studies. Hence, the title of this chapter "Elijah: A Person Like You." The difference in Elijah was not in his **genes**, but in his **faith**. He was a man who was sold out to God. He had failings. And you'll be able to identify with him along the way in some of the things that he did. But even though he was made of the same *stuff* as we

21

are, what a challenge he is to us in the way he believed God!

Secondly, he was a man who lived in the presence of God. Look at verse 1 again: "... As the Lord God of Israel liveth, before whom I stand . . . ." Elijah was living in the presence of God. He was standing in His presence and speaking with His authority. As a matter of fact, James 5:17 says, "Elijah was a man subject to like passions as we are, **and he prayed** . . . ." You see, that's the difference between Elijah and us. It's not that his nature was different than ours; it's that we have not learned to pray like he prayed. That's the difference. He was a man, but he was a man who stood in the presence of God.

Now, having noticed some things about this man, I want you to notice some things about his **motives.** Firstly, he **claimed the promises of God.** How could he say, "... there shall not be dew nor rain these years, but according to my word" (1 Ki. 17:1b)? What authority did he have to say that? Because he was claiming the promises of God. In Deuteronomy 11 is a passage with which Elijah was familiar. He based his amazing prophecy to Ahab on this promise. In Deuteronomy 11:16–17, God states: "Take heed to yourselves, that your heart be not deceived, and ye turn aside, and serve other gods, and worship them; And then the Lord's wrath be kindled against you, and he shut up the heaven, that there be no rain, and that the land yield not her fruit; and lest ye perish quickly from off the good land which the Lord giveth you." God promised that as long as they obeyed Him, He would send the rain and they would have crops. But when they turned away from Him, then He would shut up

Heaven. So when Elijah appeared before Ahab and pronounced this awful judgment of a severe drought, he was simply claiming the promise of God. The total period of this drought was three and one-half years (Jas. 5:17). Since three years passed from Elijah's prophecy until rain fell again (1 Ki. 18:1), we may assume that it had not rained for six months already. In other words, it was probably in the fall of the year — the time for the *former rains* to start falling after the dry summer. The land was already parched and yearning for rain! But Elijah then added something extra. There's not even going to be dew! Even during the dry season in Israel, there's dew on the ground in the morning. But this was to be a complete drought, resulting in famine and death — all as a judgment by God for the rampant idolatry brought in by Ahab and Jezebel!

While he claimed the promises of God, he was also concerned about the **glory of God**. "As the Lord God of Israel liveth..." (1 Ki. 17:1). In other words, if the God of Israel lives, this is going to take place. If the God of Israel does not live, then it will rain as usual. This was a contest. Ahab doubted whether the God of Israel really lived or not. Elijah said, "You want to know if God is really living? Then it is not going to rain. If God is dead, then it will rain." He was concerned for the glory of God. He said to his Lord, "Oh God, You said this in Deuteronomy 11:16 and 17. I'm concerned about Your glory. I'm willing to put my neck on the chopping block for Your glory. I'm willing to risk my reputation for Your reputation. I'm willing to do that so that You might be glorified." Throughout this series it will be seen how Elijah often did just that.

Are you willing to say, "God, Your reputation is at stake in my life. I am willing to trust You to the point of taking risks and doing things that will make Your reputation depend on me. I am willing to represent You before the world so that when people think about me or talk about me, they are thinking about my Lord. I am willing to put Your reputation at stake in my life before humanity." Elijah was a person just like you and me. But the way he differed from us was in that he was willing to do what we often are not willing to do — trust God even when it means taking a risk before others. The secret of this strength was that he lived in the presence of God. He did not quake and fear as he stood in the presence of Ahab because he knew what it was to stand in the presence of a far greater King — the Lord of Hosts. It is the practice of the presence of God that enables the child of God to stand before an unbelieving world in the boldness of fearless faith!

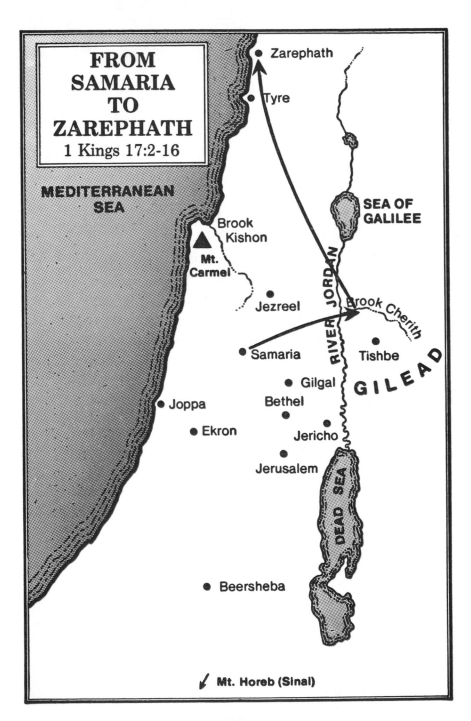

26

2

1 Kings 17: 2–16

And the word of the Lord came unto him, saying, Get thee from here, and turn thee eastward, and hide thyself by the brook, Cherith, which is before the Jordan. And it shall be, that thou shalt drink of the brook; and I have commanded the ravens to feed thee there. So he went and did according unto the word of the Lord; for he went and dwelt by the brook, Cherith, which is before the Jordan. And the ravens brought him bread and flesh in the morning, and bread and flesh in the evening, and he drank of the brook. And it came to pass after awhile, that the brook dried up, because there had been no rain in the land. And the word of the Lord came unto him, saying, Arise, get thee to Zarephath, which belongeth to Sidon, and dwell there; behold, I have commanded a widow there to sustain thee. So he arose and went to Zarephath. And when he came to the gate of the city, behold, the widow was there gathering sticks. And he called to her, and said, Fetch me, I pray thee, a little water in a vessel, that I may drink. And as she was going to fetch it, he called to her, and said, Bring me, I pray thee, a morsel of bread in thine hand. And she said, As the Lord, thy God, liveth, I have not a cake, but an handful of meal in a barrel, and a little oil in a cruse; and, behold, I am gathering two sticks, that I may go in and prepare it for me and my son, that we may eat it, and die. And Elijah said unto her, Fear not; go and do as thou hast said. But make me of it a little cake first, and bring it unto me, and, afterwards, make for thee and for thy son. For thus saith the Lord God of Israel, The barrel of meal shall not be used up, neither shall the cruse of oil fail, until the day that the Lord sendeth rain upon the earth. And she went and did according to the sayings of Elijah; and she, and he, and her house, did eat for many days. And the barrel of meal was not used up, neither did the cruse of oil fail, according to the word of the Lord, which he spoke by Elijah.

LESSONS FROM A BROOK AND A WIDOW

1 Kings 17:2–16

In the last chapter we were introduced to a man who came roaring out of the mountains of Gilead — a *rustic renegade from the rural regions*. This wild looking character marched into the palace of Ahab, pointed his bony finger at that wicked king and said, "As the Lord God lives, there's not going to be dew or rain until I say so." And just as quickly as he came in, he departed.

Ahab probably did not immediately realize that he had just been confronted with a messenger of the living God. He soon came to realize, however, that Elijah was more than a religious fanatic ranting about something of which he was ignorant.

It was autumn in Israel — the time for the *former rains* to begin falling. The next few weeks, however, witnessed the continuation of the dry season. Ahab waited a little longer — perhaps there was a delay in the seasonal cycle — but the rain did not come. It was not long before Ahab realized that he had a serious problem on his hands. Thus began a drought that would not cease for three long and dreadful years. What happened to Elijah, and where did he go during this terrible drought? The answer is given in 1 Kings 17:2–16. As soon as the drought began and the country began to suffer, God said, "Go over beyond the Jordan to a little brook named Cherith and dwell there, and I'll take care of you." He did, and God provided water from the brook and food from the ravens which brought him meat. When the brook dried up, God told him to go to a Phoenician city named Zarephath to the north of Israel. There, a widow would take care of him. So, he traveled the 80 miles and, after arriving, he met a woman who was coming out of the city. He asked for some food, but she said, "Listen we've got nothing. I'm gathering these sticks to make the fire for our last meal!" Elijah then told her, "Well, you go ahead and do that, but you will be surprised at what happens." So she did, and when she prepared the last of the meal and oil, she was amazed to find more meal in the barrel and more oil in the cruse for another meal, and then another, and then another; and for the rest of the three years, God multiplied that meal and oil so that she and her son were sustained and Elijah also.

I want you to notice four things in each of these two simple stories that teach us some amazing truths about God's ways in our personal affairs. In each of the accounts, there's a command, a promise, an obedience and a supply.

God's Command

His command was simple in the first event. "Go eastward and hide yourself by the brook Cherith." And in the second one, He said, "Get up from the brook and go to Zarephath in Sidon" — to an

isolated brook and to a town 80 miles away in the
land from which wicked Queen Jezebel came. Two
strange places. God's commands are sometimes
strange. His ways are not our ways. If we had
written the Bible, we would have written it a lot
differently. His ways are not our ways, however. He
wrote the Book and so, Elijah was commanded to
go to a brook in a very lonely place. This place was
so lonely and so desolate that geographers are not
even sure exactly where this brook is to be found on
the map. The best idea is that it was one of those
wadis that empty into the Jordan, that winding
river that today separates the *West Bank* from the
modern country of Jordan. Then Elijah was commanded to go to a lonely outpost in a foreign
country, isolated from his friends and family. Both
of the places where God commanded Elijah to go
were out of the sphere of Ahab's influence, and thus
were isolated from his wrath and the ravages of the
drought. But that was not the only reason that God
sent him away. I would suggest that the reason God
sent him away was this: **for further judgment on
Israel**. The one person whom Israel and Ahab
needed most during this time was Elijah. They
needed the voice of this prophet more now than
they ever did. The greatest need that Israel had in
the darkest hour of their existence was the voice of
a prophet, and they didn't have it. He was gone.
Proverbs 29:18 states: "Where there is no vision,
the people perish . . . ." This verse does not mean
what it is often said to mean, i.e., that unless we
have a vision for evangelism, then the lost will
perish. The word *vision* there means prophetic
vision, and where there is no prophetic vision with a

resulting message from a prophet giving guidance to the people, **then** the people perish. When there's no sure word from God, then the people starve and die. The prophet Amos warns Israel of this when he states, "Behold, the days come, saith the Lord God, that I will send a famine in the land, not a famine of bread, nor a thirst for water, but of hearing the words of the Lord" (Amos 8:11). Without a prophet in their midst, the people not only were suffering from a famine of food, but also from a famine of the word from God. So, God sent Elijah away as further judgment on Israel. Jesus recalled this incident in that fateful sermon before His home synagogue: "But I tell you of a truth, many widows were in Israel in the days of Elijah, when the heaven was shut up three years and six months, when great famine was throughout all the land; But unto none of them was Elijah sent, but only unto Zarephath, a city of Sidon, unto a woman that was a widow" (Lk. 4:25–26). Jesus declared to the people of His day that they were no better than the wicked Israelites of Elijah's day. They didn't deserve to have a prophet among them! In other words, if people do not receive the light God has given, He may very well take away even that light!

God's Promise

Attached to both of God's commands were two unfailing promises. "And it shall be, that thou shalt drink of the brook; and I have commanded the ravens to feed thee there" (17:4). "When you go, I'll take care of you," God told him. That's a promise. Then God said, "Arise, get thee to Zarephath, which belongeth to Sidon, and dwell there; behold, I have commanded a widow there to sustain thee" (17:9). That's the promise. You go; I'll meet your needs. Whenever God commands His children to do something, He also promises them the grace and means with which to do it. My dear friend, God will never ask you to do something without providing the grace and help to do it. Behind God's commands lies His omnipotence. If God has commanded you to do something, don't you dare say you can't do it. With every command of God comes a promise to aid you in obeying that command. Notice that God employed some unlikely means: small ravens and a widow. I can't think of two more unlikely means for God to use in fulfilling His promise. Ravens were unclean birds (Lev. 11:15, 20). Furthermore, can you think of a more unlikely person to meet the needs of a man during a famine and drought than a widow? In ancient times, the word *widow* was synonymous with *poverty*. The raven and the widow are examples of God's sovereignty in employing unlikely means to fulfill His promises. Oftentimes, God meets our needs in unlikely ways. F.W. Krummacher, a German pastor in the eighteenth century, relates the following in his book on the life of Elijah:

Who else was it but the God of Elijah who only a short time ago in our neighborhood delivered a poor man out of his distress and, not by a raven, but by a poor singing bird. The man was sitting early in the morning by his house door. His eyes were red with weeping. His heart cried to heaven for he was expecting an officer to come and detain him for a small debt. And while sitting

33

there with his heavy heart, a little bird flew to the street, fluttered up and down as if in distress, until at length, quick as an arrow, it flew over the good man's head into his cottage, and perched itself on an empty cupboard. The good man could little imagine who had sent the good bird, closed the door, caught the bird and placed it in a cage where it immediately began to sing very sweetly. And it seemed to the man that it was the tune of a favorite hymn . . . "Fear thou not when Darkness Reigns," an old German Lutheran hymn. As he listened, he found it soothed and comforted his mind. Suddenly, someone knocked at his door. "Ah, it's the officer," thought the man. He was terribly afraid. But no, it was the servant of a rich lady who said that the neighbors had seen a bird fly into his house, and she wished to know if he had caught it. "Oh, yes," answered the man. "Here it is." And the bird was carried away. A few minutes after, the servant came again. "You have done my mistress a great service," said he. "She sets a high value on the bird which had escaped from her, and she is much obliged to you and requests you to accept this trifle with her thanks." The poor man received it thankfully and it proved to be neither more nor less than the sum he owed. And when the officer came, he said, "Here is the amount of the debt. Now leave me in peace, for God hath sent it to me."

Now notice that God said, I'm going to "feed thee **there**" (at the brook Cherith), and "I have commanded a widow **there** [in Zarephath] to sustain thee" (17:4, 9). The promise was to meet his needs

34

only at the brook Cherith, and later only at Zarephath. Elijah had no promise that if he took off to
the Gulf of Elat, God would take care of him. The
place of God's appointment is the place of His
provision. In other words, you've got to be in the
place God wants you to be if you expect to claim the
promise that God will meet your needs. This is the
Old Testament counterpart of a New Testament
truth that's stated in Matthew 6:33: "But seek ye
first the kingdom of God, and his righteousness,
and all these things shall be added unto you." If I
am seeking first the kingdom of God, I can be
assured that God will meet my needs. The place of
God's appointment is the place of His provision.
Are you where God wants you to be? Then you can
claim God's promise that He will meet your need.

Elijah's Obedience

First Kings 17:5 and 10 states: "So he went and
did according unto the word of the Lord . . ."; and
"So he arose and went to Zarephath . . . ." His obedience was immediate; it wasn't delayed. Delayed
obedience is disobedience. Partial obedience is
disobedience. He wasn't like Saul who partly
obeyed the Lord by sparing Agag, the cattle, and
the sheep, when he was commanded to destroy
them all. Even when Saul said that he kept the
animals to sacrifice them to the Lord, Samuel told
him, ". . . Hath the Lord as great delight in burnt
offerings and sacrifices, as in obeying the voice of
the Lord? Behold, **to obey** is better than sacrifice,
and to hearken than the fat of rams" (1 Sam.
15:22).

It must have been lonely at Cherith. Ravens aren't very good conversationalists! But there were lessons that Elijah learned there that he couldn't have learned anywhere else. Before Carmel must come Cherith! Some of the greatest men of God had to spend time alone before they were used of God in a great way. After Moses' forty years of college education in Egypt, he spent forty years of graduate study in the wilderness to prepare him for his life's work! Paul had to spend three years in Arabia and a decade of silence in Tarsus before his great deeds were accomplished for God. Before Elijah stood on Mount Carmel challenging the prophets of Baal, he had to spend some time alone at the brook Cherith. So often that's true in our spiritual experiences. The discipline of loneliness teaches us things that we can never learn in the public place. My dear friend, there are lessons that you and I can learn only by the brook Cherith — lessons we can't learn anywhere else. You may be discouraged because God seemingly has not opened the doors for you in some great way. It seems that try as you may, you're still tarrying and waiting for God to open the door, but it may well be for a reason. Wait patiently for His timing in your life. Your most important responsibility is to do what God wants you to do **now**. He will take care of the future.

God's Supply

First Kings 17:6 simply states, "And the ravens brought him bread and flesh in the morning, and bread and flesh in the evening, and he drank of the brook." First Kings 17:11–16 relates the miracle of

God's providing enough meal and oil each day for the day's needs throughout Elijah's stay with the widow. The ravens were God's supernatural supply. God miraculously changed the nature of these birds so that they did not eat the meat themselves, but brought it to Elijah. Have you ever experienced any of God's ravens? If you haven't, you've never learned to live by faith. Be thankful for God's natural supply (i.e., the brook). God does not always send ravens. He expects us to scoop the water up out of the brook through our own effort. But sometimes, God sends ravens. Thank Him for that.

During my days of preparation for the ministry, after I entered college with only $200 in the bank and four years of tuition, room and board facing me, I experienced both the brook and the ravens. I worked as a waiter, an usher, a clean-up boy, and at other menial tasks to pay the bills. But, occasionally, I would be notified that some anonymous person had made a gift toward my tuition — one of God's ravens.

Then during my ministry, I regularly received a check from a bank in Philadelphia for a Christmas Club account and a Vacation Club account — accounts which I had never opened, but which had been opened in my name by one of God's ravens.

Have you experienced any of God's ravens? If you haven't I trust you will. I believe He sends them to those who, like Elijah, are willing to trust Him. You are not relieved of the responsibility of toiling and sweating for God's natural supply, but occasionally, He will send ravens to encourage you as He knows your need. He owns the cattle on a thousand hills . . . He certainly can take care of you and me!

In the early days of the Dallas Theological Seminary, there was a serious financial crisis. The crisis was such that if a large amount of money was not received on a certain day, it would seriously endanger the life of the school. In those days, the president of Dallas Seminary, Lewis Sperry Chafer, would often be visited by a great Bible teacher who taught part-time at the seminary — Dr. Harry Ironside. Dr. Ironside happened to be at the school on that crucial day of the financial deadline. Chafer and Ironside and other officials of the school gathered in Chafer's office for a prayer meeting, and they were asking God to meet the need. Ironside prayed what came to be known as one of his *famous* prayers. He said, "Oh God, You own the cattle on a thousand hills. Lord won't You sell some of those cattle and send us the money?" The secretary then came to the office and said, "There's someone here to see you, Dr. Chafer." He said, "Send him in." A Texas rancher appeared and asked, "Are you Dr. Chafer?" "Yes," Dr. Chafer replied. "Sir, I'm a cattle rancher, and I don't know what came over me, but God has told me to sell some of my cattle and give you the money." He handed Dr. Chafer the money, and the amount was exactly what was needed to alleviate the crisis!

My dear friend, if you've never experienced any of God's ravens, I hope you will, because I believe it's a token God sends us to remind us of how faithful He is to those who trust Him. Are you trusting Him?

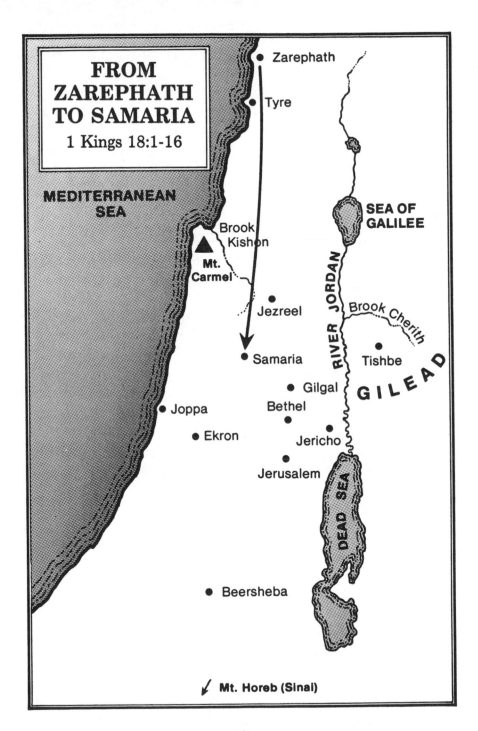

FROM
ZAREPHATH
TO SAMARIA
1 Kings 18:1-16

MEDITERRANEAN
SEA

Zarephath

Tyre

Brook
Kishon

Mt.
Carmel

Jezreel

Samaria

Gilgal

Bethel

Joppa

Ekron

Jericho

Jerusalem

Beersheba

SEA OF
GALILEE

RIVER JORDAN

Brook Cherith

Tishbe

GILEAD

DEAD SEA

Mt. Horeb (Sinai)

3
1 Kings 18:1–16

And it came to pass, after many days, that the word of the Lord came to Elijah in the third year, saying, Go, show thyself unto Ahab, and I will send rain upon the earth. And Elijah went to show himself unto Ahab. And there was a severe famine in Samaria. And Ahab called Obadiah, who was the governor of his house. (Now Obadiah feared the Lord greatly; For it was so, when Jezebel cut off the prophets of the Lord, that Obadiah took an hundred prophets, and hid them by fifty in a cave, and fed them with bread and water.) And Ahab said unto Obadiah, Go into the land, unto all fountains of water, and unto all brooks; perhaps we may find grass to save the horses and mules alive, that we lose not all the beasts. So they divided the land between them to pass throughout it: Ahab went one way by himself, and Obadiah went another way by himself. And as Obadiah was in the way, behold, Elijah met him; and he knew him, and fell on his face, and said,

Is that you, my lord Elijah? And he answered him, I am: go, tell thy lord, Behold, Elijah is here. And he said, In what have I sinned, that thou wouldest deliver thy servant into the hand of Ahab, to slay me? As the Lord, thy God, liveth, there is no nation or kingdom, where my lord hath not sent to seek thee. And when they said, He is not there, he took an oath of the kingdom and nation, that they found thee not. And now thou sayest, Go, tell thy lord, Behold, Elijah is here. And it shall come to pass, as soon as I am gone from thee, that the Spirit of the Lord shall carry thee where I know not; and so when I come and tell Ahab, and he cannot find thee, he shall slay me. But I, thy servant, fear the Lord from my youth. Was it not told my lord what I did when Jezebel slew the prophets of the Lord, how I hid an hundred men of the Lord's prophets by fifty in a cave, and fed them with bread and water? And now thou sayest, Go, tell thy lord, Behold, Elijah is here. And he shall slay me. And Elijah said, As the Lord of hosts liveth, before whom I stand, I will surely show myself unto him today. So Obadiah went to meet Ahab, and told him; and Ahab went to meet Elijah.

OBADIAH — SERVANT OF THE LORD?

1 Kings 18: 1–16

The idyllic scene in the widow's home at Zarephath stretched into months and years. Surely Elijah increasingly endeared himself to the poor woman and her son. Even when the storm clouds of death entered the home and broke over the head of the boy, Elijah's powerful intercession before God resulted in the boy's miraculous restoration. It was then that this woman, who had lived outside of the covenant people, recognized the reality of Elijah's God (1 Ki. 17:17–24).

But now a new chapter in Elijah's ministry was to unfold. The forced seclusion of three years was about to give way to a spectacular public ministry unequaled in all prophetic experience! "And it came to pass, after many days, that the word of the Lord came to Elijah in the third year, saying, Go, show thyself unto Ahab, and I will send rain upon the earth" (1 Ki. 18:1). The awful drought had run its course. The time had arrived for its cessation. But this could not take place without Elijah's showing himself openly to Ahab to announce the releasing of the judgment. Elijah had said the drought would end only at his word (1 Ki. 17:1). In other words, Elijah had inaugurated the judgment by a personal appearance to Ahab; therefore, he had to personally appear to Ahab to announce its termination.

"And Elijah went to show himself unto Ahab. And there was a severe famine in Samaria" (1 Ki. 18:2). As Elijah made the long trek back from Zarephath to his native land, he saw the severe devastation wrought by the famine! The music of the brooks was still. The green pastures carpeting the fields had given way to parched expanses. The skeletal remains of both wild and domestic animals lay scattered beside his path. Possibly the roads in the villages and towns were dotted by the stiffened corpses of the poor, who had succumbed to the horrors of thirst and hunger. Elijah was reminded that this had been brought about by the instrumentality of his prayer, and, yet, he had only claimed the promised judgment of God on His people's sins (cf. Dt. 11:16–17). Perhaps the severity of the judgment would cause the people to realize the exceeding sinfulness of sin.

At this point we are reintroduced to Ahab, the worst of the evil kings of Israel. His command to Obadiah, the steward of his household, is recorded in verse 5, "And Ahab said unto Obadiah, Go into the land, unto all fountains of water, and unto all brooks; perhaps we may find grass to save the horses and mules alive, that we lose not all the beasts."

The Corruption of Ahab

The corruption of this man can be seen, first of all, in his attitude toward the **prophets**. Whereas the main function of the priest was to represent the people to God, the main function of the prophet was to represent God to the people. He was the mouthpiece of God to Israel. His calling card always had inscribed on it, "Thus saith the Lord." Ahab, however, hated the prophets and what they stood for, i.e., the Word of the Lord. This is illustrated by the prophetic persecution mentioned in verse 4, "For it was so, when Jezebel cut off the prophets of the Lord, that Obadiah took an hundred prophets, and hid them by fifty in a cave, and fed them with bread and water." Jezebel's hatred for God's prophets was sanctioned by her weak-willed husband. When Ahab was later confronted by his prophetic nemesis, he exclaimed to Elijah, "Art thou he who troubleth Israel?" (v. 17). The prophet, faithful in delivering God's Word, will always be a thorn in the side of the wicked. In this regard Ahab's later appraisal of another prophet, Micaiah, is quite illuminating, ". . . There is yet one man, Micaiah, the son of Imlah, by whom we may inquire of the Lord. But I hate him; for he doth not prophesy good concerning me, but evil . . ." (1 Ki. 22:8).

Although it is easy for us to criticize Ahab's reaction to God's Word, we should ask ourselves the hard question, "How do **we** respond to preaching that hurts?" It is so easy to say to the preacher, "I really **enjoyed** your sermon." Frankly, I'm tired of hearing that well-meaning but waylaid comment. How often do we say, "Preacher, I didn't enjoy your sermon because it hurt me, but it stung where it was needed." Have you ever noticed the large followings that the exponents of *positive* and *possibility* *thinking* command? It is a sad commentary on our spiritual condition that we flock to musical concerts and to those speakers who make us feel good rather than to ministries that fearlessly proclaim God's truth to our needs.

Ahab's corruption is also illustrated by his attitude to the **people**. Ahab was so concerned about the horses and mules that he divided up the land with Obadiah so that he personally could make a diligent search for any remaining water sources. He was more concerned with his beasts than with his subjects! We know from archaeological and extrabiblical writings that Ahab had an extensive amount of chariots and horses. An inscription discovered in ancient Assyria informs us that Ahab appeared at Qarqar in Syria with 2,000 chariots. During the excavation of Megiddo, an ancient town fortified by Ahab, extensive ruins of horse stables complete with hitching posts and mangers were uncovered. These stables can be seen today by the modern visitor to this ancient site.

One would think that all of the severe judgments would have softened Ahab's heart. Alas, however, judgment had only hardened him. We should not forget that it is the goodness and long-suffering of God that leads us to repentance, not his wrath (cf. Rom. 2:4). How foolish, then, to think that there is a *purgatory* that will somehow *purge* away the sins of the dead. In most cases, judgment acts as sun upon clay — hardening it, not as sun upon butter — melting it.

The Courage of Obadiah

This unique individual, Obadiah, who served Ahab as "governor" of his house, surely must prompt an ambivalent response on the part of the reader. On the one hand, everyone must admire his courage. On the other hand, there must be disappointment at his compromise.

First, look at his good points. It is clearly stated by the sacred writer and by Obadiah himself that he followed the Lord. "And Ahab called Obadiah, who was the governor of his house. (Now Obadiah feared the Lord greatly" (18:3). ". . . But I, thy servant, fear the Lord from my youth" (18:12). This reverential trust of Almighty God comes as a breath of fresh air in a desert of spiritual blight. Obadiah was one of those few who had not bowed the knee to Baal in Israel (1 Ki. 19:18). He was truly a spiritual "rose among thorns." His name in Hebrew actually means "servant of the Lord." He is a classic example of the "remnant" spoken of throughout redemptive history. In the book of Romans, Paul uses his example and others to illustrate that in every age, no matter if it be the darkest, God has His people (Rom. 11:2–6). Belonging to the house of Israel by birth does not insure membership in the "Israel of God" (cf. Rom. 9:6; Gal. 6:16). Outward physical circumcision is not the most important matter in God's sight. Inward, spiritual circumcision of the heart is the mark of real Jewishness (Rom. 2:28–29). The Hebrew Christian who has looked beyond the law to its fulfillment in Jesus the Messiah constitutes the remnant today (Rom. 11:6).

Furthermore, Obadiah risked his life due to his reverential fear of Jehovah. He defended himself to Elijah with the words, "Was it not told my lord what I did when Jezebel slew the prophets of the Lord, how I hid an hundred men of the Lord's prophets by fifty in a cave, and fed them witn oread and water?" (18:13). Evidently Jezebel instituted a diabolical plan to eliminate the word of the Lord by exterminating the messengers of the Lord. Obadiah secretly spirited a hundred of these prophets to safety in two caves and sustained them out of his own pocket. These prophets were probably remnants of the *schools of prophets* which originated during the days of Samuel (cf. 1 Sam. 10:5–13). The Mount Carmel ridge is honeycombed with over 2,000 caves and would have provided the safety needed during this operation.

One cannot help but admire the courage of Obadiah displayed in this act of kindness. In this instance Obadiah's walk matched his talk, and his works illustrated his faith. Corrie Ten Boom relates the story of how a secret meeting of believers in the Soviet Union was interrupted by a group of four intruders who burst armed into the room announcing, "We are KGB agents. Anyone can leave and renounce his faith. All who choose to stay here will be shot." After a few individuals hastily departed, the four lay down their guns and said, "Brethren, we are not agents of the government. We are believers who simply want to find a congregation who love the Lord so much that they are willing to risk their lives for Him."

When Jesus said ". . . If any man will come after me, let him deny himself, and take up his cross daily, and follow me" (Lu. 9:23), He was calling us to a sacrificial commitment that may require us to risk our lives if we mean to follow Him fully

Compromise of Obadiah

Much can be seen in the character of Obadiah that is worthy of sincere praise. A discerning reading of this account, however, reveals a fatal flaw in the testimony of this man who "feared the Lord greatly" (18:3).

First of all must be noted his close involvement with Ahab. He was "the governor of his house" (18:3). Now there is certainly nothing inconsistent in a believer working for an unbeliever — this happens all the time and is evidence that we can be **in** the world and not be **of** the world. To be completely separate from unbelievers is impossible. Note what the apostle says in 1 Corinthians 5:9–10, "I wrote unto you in an epistle not to company with fornicators; Yet not altogether with the fornicators of this world, or with the covetous, or extortioners, or with idolators, for then must ye needs go out of the world."

Ahab's house, however, must have been a special case. The reader should keep in mind what the divine testimony was about this king: "But there was none like unto Ahab, who did sell himself to work wickedness in the sight of the Lord, whom Jezebel, his wife, stirred up" (1 Ki. 21:25). Ahab was the worst of a bad line of godless, wicked, and worthless kings. Certainly the crimes, the intrigue, and the idolatry marking his reign must have constantly infiltrated the palace. To be governor of such a palace must have certainly involved Obadiah in these matters. If he was able to avoid direct participation in this filth, evidently he raised no protest against it — or he would have lost his job, his head, or both! Furthermore, Ahab's wicked wife, Jezebel, must have introduced her vile Phoenician worship of Baal into the royal house. How could Obadiah not be involved at least indirectly in idolatry if he was the "majordomo" in Jezebel's house?

One writer on the life of Ahab zealously attempts to defend Obadiah against any charge of compromise. He cites the cases of Joseph and Daniel as being two godly examples who served in the governments of pagan kings. Joseph and Daniel, however, were exiles in the lands of Egypt and Babylon serving pagan rulers who knew nothing better than idolatry. Obadiah evidently chose to be involved in the government of Ahab, a Jewish king who should be expected to know more than pagans. Furthermore, both Joseph and Daniel suffered when they refused to be involved in the sinful activities of their bosses (cf. Gen. 39:7–20 and Dan. 6). No word is given regarding Obadiah's protest against Ahab's programs. In Obadiah there is a classic example of the "unequal yoke" (Dt. 22:10; Amos 3:3; 2 Cor. 6:14–16). It is also interesting to note that evidently Obadiah did not impress Elijah with his spirituality since Elijah later said he was the only one left who followed the Lord (19:10).

Telling evidence of the effects of Obadiah's compromise is seen in the extreme fear he had of his master. Note Obadiah's words in his exchange with Elijah. "And as Obadiah was in the way, behold, Elijah met him; and he knew him, and fell on his face, and said, Is that you, my lord Elijah? And he answered him, I am: go, tell thy lord, Behold, Elijah is here. And he said, In what have I sinned, that thou wouldest deliver thy servant into the hand of Ahab, to slay me? As the Lord, thy God, liveth, there is no nation or kingdom, where my lord hath not sent to seek thee. And when they said, He is not there, he took an oath of the kingdom and nation, that they found thee not. And now thou sayest, Go, tell thy lord, Behold, Elijah is here. And it shall come to pass, as soon as I am gone from thee, that the Spirit of the Lord shall carry thee where I know not; and so when I come and tell Ahab, and he cannot find thee, he shall slay me. But I, thy servant, fear the Lord from my youth. Was it not told my lord what I did when Jezebel slew the prophets of the Lord, how I hid an hundred men of the Lord's prophets by fifty in a cave, and fed them with bread and water? And now thou sayest, Go, tell thy lord, Behold, Elijah is here. And he shall slay me. And Elijah said, As the Lord of hosts liveth, before whom I stand, I will surely show myself unto him today. So Obadiah went to meet Ahab, and told him; and Ahab went to meet Elijah" (18:7–16). Are these the words of a fearless and stalwart servant of God? They sound more like the confession of a "secret believer" who is afraid of being discovered. The compromise of Obadiah had so weakened his testimony that he was unwilling to implicitly trust the word of Elijah. Only after Elijah assured him with an oath that he would not depart did Obadiah confront his master with the news that Elijah had arrived. The brother of our Lord reminds us, "A double-minded man is unstable in all his ways" (Jas. 1:8). Obadiah's dual allegiance to both Ahab and the Lord had resulted in spiritual instability.

Obadiah is so typical of many of God's people who today find themselves in compromising affiliations with the servants of the wicked one. In ecumenical apostate churches there are many true believers who refuse to recognize this "unequal yoke," and remain in the apostasy, thinking they can reform it from within, as if a good apple in a barrel can restore the rotten apples! The command to these and all others involved in humanistic religious systems is the call issued in Revelation 18:4: "And I heard another voice from heaven, saying, Come out of her, my people, that ye be not partakers of her sins, and that ye receive not of her plagues."

Yes, Obadiah "feared the Lord greatly," but how much greater would have been his influence had he refused to be "unequally yoked" together with Ahab! Discerning readers of these words will apply them by making sure that they are not involved in entangling alliances that will eventually compromise their testimony and limit the spiritual growth of them and their family. Membership in a sound, Bible-believing church is the place to begin.

"And have no fellowship with the unfruitful works of darkness, but, rather, reprove them" (Eph. 5:11).

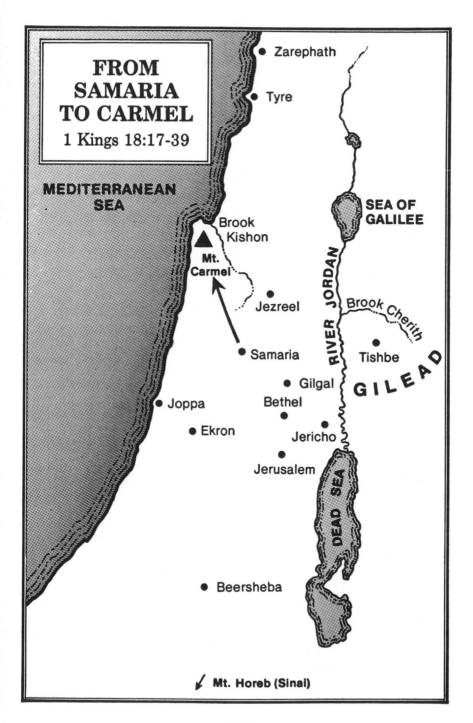

FROM
SAMARIA
TO CARMEL
1 Kings 18:17-39

MEDITERRANEAN
SEA

Zarephath

Tyre

Brook
Kishon

Mt.
Carmel

SEA OF
GALILEE

Jezreel

Brook Cherith

RIVER JORDAN

Samaria

Tishbe

GILEAD

Gilgal

Bethel

Joppa

Ekron

Jericho

Jerusalem

DEAD SEA

Beersheba

↙ Mt. Horeb (Sinai)

4

1 Kings 18:17–39

And it came to pass, when Ahab saw Elijah, that Ahab said unto him, Art thou he who troubleth Israel? And he answered, I have not troubled Israel; but thou, and thy father's house, in that ye have forsaken the commandments of the Lord, and thou hast followed Baalim. Now, therefore, send, and gather to me all Israel unto Mount Carmel, and the prophets of Baal, four hundred and fifty, and the prophets of the idols, four hundred, who eat at Jezebel's table. So Ahab sent unto all the children of Israel, and gathered the prophets together unto Mount Carmel. And Elijah came unto all the people, and said, How long halt ye between two opinions? If the Lord be God, follow him; but if Baal, then follow him. And the people answered him not a word. Then said Elijah unto the people, I, even I only, remain a prophet of the Lord; but Baal's prophets are four hundred and fifty men. Let them, therefore, give us two bullocks; and let them choose one bullock for themselves, and cut it in pieces, and lay it on wood, and put no fire under it; and I will prepare the other bullock, and lay it on wood, and put no fire under it. And call ye on the name of your gods, and I will call on the name of the Lord; and the God who answereth by fire, let him be God. And all the people answered and said, It is well spoken. And Elijah said unto the prophets of Baal, Choose you one bullock for yourselves, and prepare it first; for ye are many. And call on the name of your gods, but put no fire under it. And they took the bullock which was given them, and they prepared it, and called on the name of Baal from morning even until noon, saying, O Baal, hear us. But there was no voice, nor any that answered. And they leaped upon the altar which was made. And it came to pass at noon, that Elijah mocked them, and said, Cry aloud; for he is a god. Either he is talking, or he is pursuing, or he is in a journey, or, perhaps, he sleepeth, and must be awakened. And they cried aloud, and cut themselves after their manner with swords and lances, till the blood gushed out upon them. And it came to pass, when midday was past, and they prophesied until the time of the offering of the evening sacrifice, that there was neither voice, nor any to answer, nor any that regarded. And Elijah said unto all the people, Come near unto me. And all the people came near unto him. And he repaired the altar of the Lord that was broken down. And Elijah took twelve stones, according to the number of the tribes of the sons of Jacob, unto whom the word of the Lord came, saying, Israel shall be thy name. And with the stones he built an altar in the name of the Lord; and he made a trench about the altar, as great as would contain two measures of seed. And he put the wood in order, and cut the bullock in pieces, and laid it on the wood, and said, Fill four barrels with water, and pour it on the burnt sacrifice, and on the wood. And he said, Do it the second time. And they did it the second time. And he said, Do it the third time. And they did it the third time. And the water ran round about the altar; and he filled the trench also with water. And it came to pass at the time of the offering of the evening sacrifice, that Elijah, the prophet, came near, and said, Lord God of Abraham, Isaac, and of Israel, let it be known this day that thou art God in Israel, and that I am thy servant, and that I have done all these things at thy word. Hear me, O Lord, hear me, that this people may know that thou art the Lord God, and that thou hast turned their heart back again. Then the fire of the Lord fell, and consumed the burnt sacrifice, and the wood, and the stones, and the dust, and licked up the water that was in the trench. And when all the people saw it, they fell on their faces, and they said, The Lord, he is God; the Lord, he is God.

THE CONTEST ON CARMEL
1 Kings 18:17–39

There were two kinds of Old Testament prophets: prophets of words and prophets of deeds. Of the former, the greatest is doubtless Isaiah. Of the latter, there has not been a greater than Elijah. Isaiah gave a message to Israel through his words. Elijah spoke to Israel primarily through his deeds. Elijah was a man of action rather than diction. His experience with the prophets of Baal on Mount Carmel was probably the greatest of all his stirring deeds. Here Elijah is seen at his best.

"And it came to pass, after many days, that the word of the Lord came to Elijah in the third year, saying, Go, show thyself unto Ahab, and I will send rain upon the earth" (18:1). The moment had arrived. Baal, supposedly the god of storm and good crops, had proven utterly powerless to relieve the drought that had afflicted Israel for three and a half years (Jas. 5:17). The man of God, however, had been sustained through the Lord's supernatural provision at the brook Cherith and in the widow's home (17:2–24). It was now time for Elijah to confront Ahab again. This second confrontation would answer in a spectacular way, once and for all, the question as to who was the true and living God — the Lord or Baal. In modern parlance, one might say that it would be a match to decide who was the real *heavyweight champion of the world.*

The Call To Carmel

The scene for the great confrontation is set in 1 Kings 18:17–19. Elijah's challenge to Ahab was that he should gather all the false prophets under the throne's employment to Mount Carmel — a high ridge jutting out into the Mediterranean near modern-day Haifa. When the four hundred and fifty prophets of Baal had gathered, along with a large contingent from all the children of Israel, Elijah issued an ultimatum: ". . . How long halt ye between two opinions? If the Lord be God, follow him; but if Baal, then follow him . . ." (18:21). A literal translation of the Hebrew text is: "How long will you continue to hobble between the two forks of the road?"

The basic problem of the Israelites was not that they had totally rejected the Lord and followed Baal, but that they wanted both the Lord **and** Baal! This practice of combining Baal worship and Jehovah worship is called **syncretism**, which Webster's defines as "the attempt to combine differing beliefs." Syncretism has always had a deadening effect on the work of God. A missionary in Japan for many years relates that it is a common practice among Buddhists in that country to *receive Jesus* and simply add Him to the *god shelf* in their homes. In other words, Jesus is then worshiped along with the other gods of the Buddhist pantheon! Elijah made it clear, however, that the Lord is a jealous God who allows no rivals to His worship. The people had to make up their minds. They could not worship both the Lord and Baal. It would actually be preferable to follow Baal totally than seek to mingle the worship of that false deity with the worship of the only true God. When Christ spoke to the Laodicean church, He put the matter this way: "I know thy works, that thou art neither cold nor hot; I would thou wert cold or hot. So, then, because thou art lukewarm, and neither cold nor hot, I will spew thee out of my mouth" (Rev. 3:15–16). Some people drink hot coffee and some people drink iced coffee, but lukewarm coffee makes them both sick! The same holds true in spiritual matters.

A politician was once asked, "Are you for this issue?" In the true manner of a politician, he replied, "Well, some of my friends are for this issue, and some are against it . . . and I am for my friends!" How sad that many *professors* of religion are like these confused children of Israel. Some feel that they can live with one foot in the Kingdom of God and one in the kingdom of the world. Someone has said, "Don't sit on the fence, or you'll get shot at from both sides!"

Elijah's call to the people of Israel was to make up their minds whom they would serve. God calls us today as He did through an earlier man of God, ". . . choose you this day whom ye will serve . . ." and may we respond as he did, ". . . but as for me and my house, we will serve the Lord" (Josh. 24:15).

The Confrontation With The Prophets

Elijah threw down the gauntlet to the prophets of

Baal. The terms of the contest were to be a veritable trial by fire! The prophets were to choose a bullock, cut it in pieces, lay it on the wood of the altar, while Elijah did the same with a second bullock (18:23). They were then to proceed to implore Baal to send fire upon their altar. Elijah would do the same, but call on the Lord instead. "... and the God who answereth by fire, let him be God ..." (18:24). The people who were watching agreed that the terms were fair, so the match began!

The Baal prophets had their turn first. Throughout the morning hours they cried out for Baal to answer their increasingly frenzied entreaties, even leaping bodily on the altar to emphasize their frantic supplications. But the heavens were silent. Elijah even engaged in some *holy mockery* by poking fun at their nonexistent *god*. He reminded them that maybe Baal was hard of hearing, or maybe he was talking to someone else, or maybe he was on vacation. Worse yet, this *mighty god* possibly was tired and was enjoying a siesta (18:27)! The reader might wonder if such taunting was tactful on Elijah's part, but the prophet was only pointing out the absurdity of idolatry compared to the omnipresent, omnipotent and omniscient LORD whose ears are always open to His children's cries. God himself laughs at the foolish ideas of the heathen (Ps. 2:4) and points out vividly in other passages the absolute idiocy of worshiping dumb and deaf objects as so-called *gods*. Consider for example the "holy sarcasm" of Psalm 115:4–8: "Their idols are silver and gold, the work of men's hands. They have mouths, but they speak not; eyes have they, but they see not. They have ears, but they hear not; noses have they, but they smell not. They have hands, but they handle not; feet have they, but they walk not; neither speak they through their throat. They who make them are like unto them; so is every one who trusteth in them."

Elijah's biting satire only drove the frantic devotees into a greater frenzy — they cut their own bodies with knives, thinking that perhaps Baal would then have pity on them because of their suffering. They continued thus to the middle of the afternoon, but when they finally dropped in exhaustion, ". . . there was neither voice, nor any to answer, nor any that regarded" (18:29).

The misguided actions of the prophets serve to remind us of a very important truth. Faith and sincerity in religious worship do not insure that one's worship is acceptable. No one could deny that they had faith! No one could fault them for not being sincere! The only problem is that their faith was in the **wrong** object and they were sincerely **wrong**! It is not enough to have faith — faith is only as good as its object. It is not enough to be sincere. Jesus reminded the Samaritan woman that true worship of God must not be only sincere, it must be ". . . in spirit and in **truth**" (Jn. 4:24). The Apostle Paul did not fault the sincerity of his unbelieving Jewish brethren, but their zeal did not merit salvation. "For I bear them witness that they have a zeal for God, but not according to knowledge. For they, being ignorant of God's righteousness, and going about to establish their own righteousness, have not submitted themselves unto the righteousness of God" (Rom. 10:2–3). How true is the old saying, "The road to Hell is paved with good intentions."

The Confirmation By Jehovah

The ball was now in Elijah's court. His calm, measured approach contrasted boldly with the frantic actions of the prophets. First, he rebuilt the broken down altar of the Lord with twelve stones, according to the twelve tribes of Israel, also adding a trench about the new altar (18:30–32). Secondly, he arranged the bullock in pieces on the wood and then ordered that twelve barrels of water be poured on the sacrifice, filling the trench as well. If someone should question where twelve barrels of precious water could be gotten during a drought, he should remember that the abundant salt waters of the Mediterranean are at the foot of Mount Carmel. By this thorough drenching, Elijah wanted to make sure that no one would think that the coming miracle was only performed through some *trick* on his part. Thirdly, he prayed. The prayer was simple, direct and centered on the honor of God.

> ... *Lord God of Abraham, Isaac, and of Israel, let it be known this day that thou art God in Israel, and that I am thy servant, and that I have done all these things at thy word. Hear me, O Lord, hear me, that this people may know that thou art the Lord God, and that thou hast turned their heart back again (18:36–37).*

Just as God responded to Solomon's prayer at the dedication of the Temple (2 Chr. 7:1), so He responded to Elijah. "Then the fire of the Lord fell, and consumed the burnt sacrifice, and the wood, and the stones, and the dust, and licked up the water that was in the trench" (18:38).

The effect of this magnificent display was a unanimous decision on the part of the judges: "And when all the people saw it, they fell on their faces, and they said, The Lord, he is God; the Lord, he is God" (18:39). No one could dispute the decision. Baal had been shown to be a nonexistent impostor! The Lord God of the Hebrews had vindicated His prophet, who had risked not just his own reputation but the reputation of his God as well.

Dr. Richard Harvey related the following true experience in the January, 1975 issue of **Moody Monthly** which should serve well to apply this incident to our lives.

Three periods before the Thanksgiving holiday our chemistry professor always planned to lecture against prayer. He was so sarcastic, and so ridiculed prayer that he used to have the kids in stitches. Then every year at the close of his first lecture he would say, "By the way, is there anybody here who still believes in prayer?" He would then step in front of his lecture table and hold up a two-quart glass flask. There was a concrete floor in the classroom. Then he would say: "Now, if there's anybody here who believes in prayer, I'm going to ask you to stand and pray that when I drop this flask it won't break. Now I want you to know, students, that all of your prayers and the prayers of your parents and those of your Sunday school teachers and those of your pastors (and I'm willing for you to bring them all here to pray with you) — not all their prayers, nothing, can keep that flask from breaking when I let it go." He had been doing this for fifteen years. Talk about Goliath!

When I was a senior a certain freshman came to the school. One day there was a knock at my door. I opened it and there stood this freshman. He said, "Are you Dick Harvey?"

"Yes," I said.

"Well, some of the upperclassmen told me that you were the only fellow in this school who believes in prayer. I want you to understand that I'm a born-again Christian. I'm majoring in chemistry — which is perhaps a foolish thing for me to do since I know what Dr. Lee does. But God has shown me that He wants me to stand up to him. Now I want you to pray that God will give me courage when the time comes and I also want you to pray that the flask won't break. I would appreciate it if every time you pray you would ask God about this, even when you say grace at the table. I've only a couple of weeks before Dr. Lee will be doing this and I want God to give me the courage to stand up to him."

"All right," I said, "I'll pray with you."

Well, I was majoring in chemistry because I intended to go to medical school following my college work. I was downstairs in the qualitative analysis laboratory when the lecture hour came. About the time I knew Dr. Lee would defy prayer I went upstairs and stood in the back of the auditorium. My heart was full of fear; I was actually shaking. If you had been near me you would have thought I had palsy. Finally he came to the moment. Out in front he stepped and he said, "Now is there anyone here who still

64

believes in prayer?" The young fellow was sitting near the middle of the big auditorium. He stood right up and stepped into the aisle, "Dr. Lee," he said, "I do."

"My, this is real interesting, isn't it?" Dr. Lee said. "We've got a fellow here who believes that God can answer prayer! Maybe I'd better explain to you again what I am going to do." He went through the whole procedure: how he would hold up the flask, open his hand and let it drop. It would go into hundreds of pieces, he said, and there wasn't any power in the world or in heaven that would stop that flask from breaking. After he finished his speech, he turned to the young man and asked, "Do you still want to pray?"

The young man said, "Yes, Dr. Lee, I do."

"Well," he said, "isn't that interesting? Now we'll all be real reverent while this young man prays."

The young man did not even bow his head; he just lifted his eyes toward heaven and said, "Dear Heavenly Father, in the name of Jesus, I thank You and You have heard me. For your honor and Christ's name sake and for the honor of your servant who puts his trust in you, don't let this flask break. Amen."

Dr. Lee took the flask, held it out, opened his hand and as it fell God changed its course. He drew it in. Instead of falling straight down, it hit the toe of Dr. Lee's shoe and rolled over.

And it did not break!

The class gave Dr. Lee the hee-haw, and all the rest of the time he was there he never lectured *on prayer. God ended that once and for all. Even though it happened many years ago, the story of the flask that wouldn't break is still told on the campus of that school.*

Elijah was willing to stand up for his God and his God vindicated Himself and His prophet before an observing world. Are you willing to risk the jeers and taunts of others by standing up today for the Lord God of Elijah? You may never stand on Mount Carmel, but you will be called to stand up for the Lord in situations that demand the courage of Elijah. As you are faithful to Him, He certainly will be faithful to you.

"Because he hath set his love upon me, therefore will I deliver him; I will set him on high, because he hath known my name" (Ps. 91:14). ". . . them who honor me I will honor . . ." (1 Sam. 2:30).

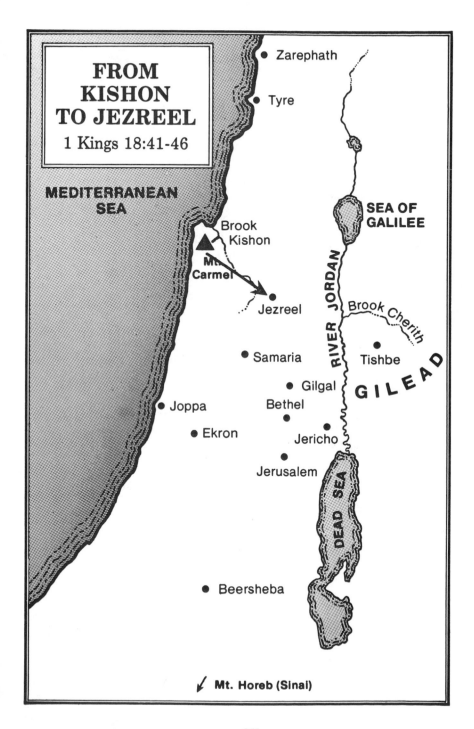

FROM
KISHON
TO JEZREEL
1 Kings 18:41-46

MEDITERRANEAN
SEA

Zarephath

Tyre

SEA OF
GALILEE

Brook
Kishon

Mt.
Carmel

RIVER JORDAN

Jezreel

Brook Cherith

Samaria

Tishbe

GILEAD

Gilgal

Bethel

Joppa

Ekron

Jericho

Jerusalem

DEAD SEA

Beersheba

↙ Mt. Horeb (Sinal)

5

1 Kings 18:41–46

And Elijah said unto Ahab, Get thee up, eat and drink; for there is a sound of abundance of rain. So Ahab went up to eat and to drink. And Elijah went up to the top of Carmel; and he cast himself down upon the earth, and put his face between his knees, And said to his servant, Go up now, look toward the sea. And he went up, and looked, and said, There is nothing. And he said, Go again seven times. And it came to pass at the seventh time, that he said, Behold, there ariseth a little cloud out of the sea, like a man's hand. And he said, Go up, say unto Ahab, Prepare thy chariot, and get thee down, that the rain stop thee not. And it came to pass in the meanwhile, that the heaven was black with clouds and wind, and there was a great rain. And Ahab rode, and went to Jezreel. And the hand of the Lord was on Elijah; and he girded up his loins, and ran before Ahab to the entrance of Jezreel.

ELIJAH
AND THE RAIN

1 Kings 18:41–46

After most ministers finish their sermons, both preacher and congregation leave to eat a meal. It has often been said that since most Christians don't drink and smoke, their biggest vice is eating. It is instructive to note the actions of Ahab and Elijah following the confrontation on Carmel. The prophets of Baal had been shown to be false prophets when their *god* had been deaf to their prayers. They suffered the fate of false prophets when Elijah personally put them to death at the Brook Kishon (cf. Dt. 13:5). "And Elijah said unto them, Take the prophets of Baal; let not one of them escape. And they took them. And Elijah brought them down to the brook, Kishon, and slew them there" (1 Ki. 18:40). Following this amazing display of God's power and justice, Ahab goes to eat while Elijah goes to pray. "And Elijah said unto Ahab, Get thee up, eat and drink; for there is a sound of abundance of rain. So Ahab went up to eat and to drink. And Elijah went up to the top of Carmel; and he cast himself down upon the earth, and put his face between his knees" (1 Ki. 18:41–42).

How stark is the contrast between the actions of the wicked king and the prophet. As a matter of fact

Elijah actually told Ahab to eat and drink! Evidently Ahab had not joined with the people in acknowledging that the LORD was the true God (v. 39). No doubt he stood by as his hireling prophets were humiliated and then executed. Elijah did not even give him any further exhortation to report. The reason for this is found in the description of the moral character of the king in 1 Kings 21:25, "But there was none like unto Ahab, who did sell himself to work wickedness in the sight of the Lord, whom Jezebel, his wife, stirred up." It is useless to expostulate with an apostate. The prophet understood the character of Ahab very well. He knew the hardness and insensibility of his heart so he told him to do only that which he was capable of doing — fulfilling his physical desires. A parallel to this command can be found in the words of the Lord Jesus to the traitor Judas in John 13:27, "And after the sop Satan entered into him. Then said Jesus unto him, What thou doest, do quickly."

The contrasting behavior of Elijah is striking. So far from thinking of his own physical needs, which at this point no doubt were great, Elijah gave himself to prayer. A. W. Pink expressed it well when he wrote, "Ahab hastens to his carnal feast, but the Tishbite, like his Lord, has 'meat to eat' which others knew not of, John 4:32."

It is good to notice at this point the importance of prayer in the recorded ministry of Elijah. When James, the brother of the Lord Jesus, made his reference to Elijah he noted this example of his prayer life: "Elijah was a man subject to like passions as we are, and he prayed earnestly that it might not rain; and it rained not on the earth by the space of three years and six months. And he prayed again, and the heaven gave rain, and the earth brought forth her fruit" (Jas. 5:17–18). He used Elijah's example to illustrate the truth he had stated, "The effectual, fervent prayer of a righteous man availeth much" (Jas. 5:16b). Tradition records that James prayed so much that his knees were as tough as a camel's. Evidently he felt a spiritual kinship to his prophetic predecessor. It is mentioned that Elijah prayed to begin the drought (cf. 1 Ki. 17:1 and Jas. 5:17). Elijah later offered a simple yet fervent prayer for the recovery of the widow's son in Zarephath (1 Ki. 17:20–22). On Mount Carmel Elijah offered a simple yet bold prayer to the God of Abraham, Isaac, and Israel to show Himself as the true God (1 Ki. 18:36–37). Even in his depression he cried out to the Lord under the juniper tree in the wilderness — the only prayer of Elijah which God did not grant (1 Ki. 19:4). The final recorded prayer of Elijah is the calling down of fiery judgment on the messengers of Ahaziah who was seeking the help of the pagan god Baalzebub (2 Ki. 1:2–12). The obvious lesson to the modern servant of God is that our public ministry with men will only be as powerful as our private ministry with God.

In this regard it is instructive to notice the reason Elijah gave for urgency of his instruction to Ahab, ". . . for there is a sound of abundance of rain" (v. 41b). It is obvious from the context that there was a cloudless sky at the time. Even after the initial praying of Elijah, his servant told him that there was nothing in the sky (v. 43). The *sound* that Elijah heard fell on deaf ears to Ahab. The ear of faith hears what the eye of flesh cannot see. Hebrews 11:1 declares, "Now faith is the substance of things hoped for, the evidence of things not seen." A legitimate paraphrase of that famous text could be expressed in this way, "Faith looks upon things promised as though they were already fulfilled." Elijah was so confident that God was going to answer his prayer that the storm was already rumbling in his ears!

The Earnestness Of His Prayer

With his face between his knees on the soil of Mount Carmel, Elijah sought the Lord. Unlike the other prayers that are mentioned in his ministry, the actual words he expressed to God are not recorded. His silent posture is an eloquent testimony to his earnestness. No specific instruction as to the physical manner of prayer is given in the Bible. There are examples in the Bible of people praying while standing (Neh. 9:5), kneeling (Ezra 9:5), sitting (1 Chr. 17:16), bowing (Ex. 34:8), and with uplifted hands (1 Tim. 2:8). All that can be said of Elijah's posture was that it was outward evidence of his inward earnestness. The physical position of his body was a reflection of the spiritual attitude of his heart.

In taking notice of Elijah's praying, it is good to ask the question, "Why did Elijah believe that he needed to pray at all?" Had not God given the explicit promise previously in 1 Kings 18:1, "And it came to pass, after many days, that the word of the Lord came to Elijah in the third year, saying, Go, show thyself unto Ahab, and I will send rain upon

72

the earth"? If God had already stated what He would do, why pray? It is here that we encounter those two seemingly contradictory truths that permeate the Bible — the sovereignty of God and the responsibility of man. While God is the sovereign planner of events and is not surprised or thwarted by human deeds or misdeeds, man is still a creature endowed with choice and responsibility. These two apparently irreconcilable truths come together in the following proposition: God has ordained the means as well as the ends. Yes, God had ordained the ends, i.e., that rain would be sent, but He also had ordained the means, that the rain would be sent in response to Elijah's prayer. How much confusion would be avoided if believers could bring themselves to accept **both** the sovereignty of God and the responsibility of man. How many heated arguments would be cooled! Yes, it is true that God has chosen some to salvation (Eph. 1:3–6). It is also true that those chosen ones will come to salvation through our prayerful preaching of the gospel (Mt. 28:19). Both of these truths are balanced in 2 Thessalonians 2:13–14, "But we are bound to give thanks always to God for you, brethren beloved of the Lord, because God hath from the beginning chosen you to salvation through sanctification of the Spirit and belief of the truth, Unto which he called you by our gospel, to the obtaining of the glory of our Lord Jesus Christ."

The sovereignty of God does not relieve us of the responsibility to pray. It has been said that prayer is the hand of faith that translates promise into performance. As a matter of fact, it was the sovereign purpose of God that enabled Elijah to

73

pray with such earnestness!

The Expectation Of His Prayer

"And [he] said to his servant, Go up now, look toward the sea. And he went up, and looked, and said, There is nothing. And he said, Go again seven times. And it came to pass at the seventh time, that he said, Behold, there ariseth a little cloud out of the sea, like a man's hand. And he said, Go up, say unto Ahab, Prepare thy chariot, and get thee down, that the rain stop thee not" (1 Ki. 18:43–44). Elijah not only prayed earnestly, he prayed expectantly. When the servant initially saw no indication in the sky of a coming rain storm, the prophet simply told him to keep looking — it would eventually appear. When the servant returned again without sighting any indication of rain, Elijah told him to look again. To Elijah, the question was not if, but only **when**. He prayed expecting God to answer. In regard to prayer it is important to realize that if you expect nothing, you will seldom be disappointed. Jesus said that if we are to be given anything, we must ask for it; if we are to have the door opened to us, we must knock; and if we are to find our answers, we must seek for them (Mt. 7:7). The verb tenses in that precious promise should be noted. Jesus actually said, "Keep on asking, keep on seeking, and keep on knocking." How impatient is the Christian who is disappointed when God does not grant his request right away! This same believer is often surprised when God does answer quickly!

The experience of Peter's deliverance from prison in Acts 12:5–16 illustrates this truth in a

74

humorous way. "Peter, therefore, was kept in prison; but prayer was made without ceasing by the church unto God for him" (Acts 12:5). When God miraculously delivered Peter (in response to their prayers) he appeared before the door of the assembled believers even while they were still praying inside. When the young girl told the news to them that Peter was outside waiting to come in, they thought she was mad. When they finally let him in "they were astonished" (Acts 12:16). If they had really been praying expectantly, should they have been astonished? In 1976 I was stricken with viral encephalitis. The congregation of which I was the pastor prayed diligently for my recovery. When I made a quick recovery and appeared the following Sunday, a number expressed surprise that I was back so quickly. My response was, "Why are you surprised? Didn't you pray expecting my recovery?"

Elijah prayed expectantly. When the little cloud appeared he knew that the time for the answer had arrived. He had never doubted **that** it would come.

The Effect of His Prayer

Even though Ahab was wicked, he was still the king. Out of respect to that position, Elijah warned him to get moving before he was overtaken by the raging storm about to burst over the Carmel and the Valley of Jezreel. Elijah knew that the Brook Kishon would be swollen and might endanger Ahab even as had taken place to the soldiers of Sisera (cf. Jud. 5:19–21).

The effect of Elijah's prayer was twofold: (1) on the land, and (2) on himself. The rain descended in torrents. "And it came to pass in the meanwhile, that the heaven was black with clouds and wind, and there was a great rain. And Ahab rode, and went to Jezreel" (1 Ki. 18:45). Three and a half years of drought were ended. Rain is often mentioned in the Bible as a blessing of God (e.g., Lev. 26:4; Ps. 147:8). Yet, God had withheld the blessing because of national sin. When the nation acknowledged its sin, God responded with the blessing of rain. It is in this context that the oft misunderstood statement of God to Solomon should be understood. "And the Lord appeared to Solomon by night, and said unto him, I have heard thy prayer, and have chosen this place for myself as an house of sacrifice. If I shut up heaven that there is no rain, or if I command the locusts to devour the land, or if I send pestilence among my people; If my people, who are called by my name, shall humble themselves, and pray, and seek my face, and turn from their wicked ways, then will I hear from heaven, and will forgive their sin, and will heal their land" (2 Chr. 7:12–14).

Elijah's prayer was effective, not because of its **language**, nor because of its **length**, nor because of its **loudness**. His prayer was effective because it was earnest, expectant, and based on God's promises.

The final effect of the prayer was on Elijah himself. "And the hand of the Lord was on Elijah; and he girded up his loins, and ran before Ahab to the entrance of Jezreel" (1 Ki. 18:46). God honored his prophet by a supernatural enabling to also escape the torrent. He actually outran Ahab's chariot the entire eight miles to Jezreel! Elijah would not have *hitched a ride* with Ahab even if he had been invited. The prophet had horsepower which the king had never dreamed of!

Elijah's prayer was earnest, expectant, and effective. Pastors bemoan the fact that they can get their people to do almost anything but pray. They will come to socials, banquets, even to hear good preaching, but very rarely will they come to pray! Perhaps it is because they don't really believe that it works. Perhaps they prayed for something and nothing happened. How thankful I am that my godly grandparents never stopped praying for a wayward grandson. They prayed earnestly and expectantly and their prayer was effective. Keep asking, keep seeking and keep knocking.

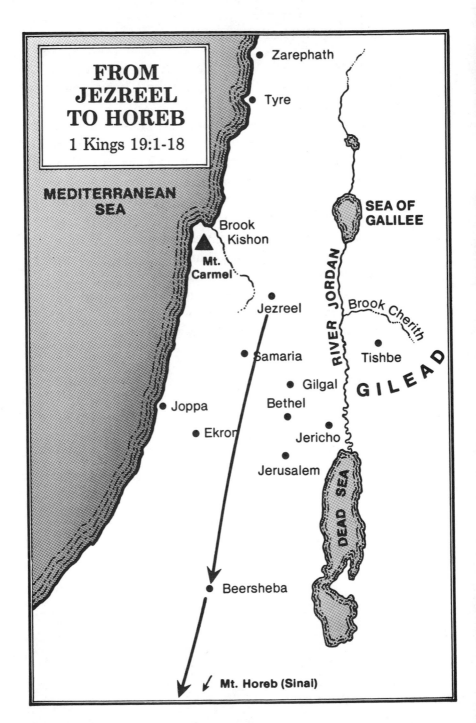

FROM
JEZREEL
TO HOREB
1 Kings 19:1-18

MEDITERRANEAN
SEA

Zarephath

Tyre

SEA OF
GALILEE

Brook
Kishon

Mt.
Carmel

Jezreel

RIVER JORDAN

Brook Cherith

Samaria

Tishbe

GILEAD

Gilgal

Bethel

Joppa

Ekron

Jericho

Jerusalem

DEAD SEA

Beersheba

Mt. Horeb (Sinai)

6
1 Kings 19:1–18

*And Ahab told Jezebel all that Elijah had done,
and how he had slain all the prophets with the sword.
Then Jezebel sent a messenger unto Elijah, saying,
So let the gods do to me, and more also, if I make not
thy life as the life of one of them by tomorrow about
this time. And when he saw that, he arose, and went
for his life, and came to Beer-sheba, which belongeth
to Judah, and left his servant there. But he himself
went a day's journey into the wilderness, and came
and sat down under a juniper tree. And he requested
for himself that he might die, and said, It is enough!
Now, O Lord, take away my life; for I am not better
than my fathers. And as he lay and slept under a
juniper tree, behold, an angel touched him, and said
unto him, Arise and eat. And he looked, and, behold,
there was a cake baked on the coals, and a cruse of
water at his head. And he did eat and drink, and lay
down again. And the angel of the Lord came again
the second time, and touched him, and said, Arise
and eat, because the journey is too great for thee. And
he arose, and did eat and drink, and went in the
strength of that food forty days and forty nights unto
Horeb, the mount of God. And he came there unto a
cave, and lodged there; and, behold, the word of the
Lord came to him, and he said unto him, What doest
thou here, Elijah? And he said, I have been very
jealous for the Lord God of hosts. For the children of
Israel have forsaken thy covenant, thrown down*

thine altars, and slain thy prophets with the sword; and I, even I only, am left, and they seek my life, to take it away. And he said, Go forth, and stand upon the mount before the Lord. And, behold, the Lord passed by, and a great and strong wind rent the mountains, and broke in pieces the rocks before the Lord; but the Lord was not in the wind. And after the wind an earthquake; but the Lord was not in the earthquake. And after the earthquake a fire; but the Lord was not in the fire. And after the fire a still, small voice. And it was so, when Elijah heard it, that he wrapped his face in his mantle, and went out, and stood in the entrance of the cave. And, behold, there came a voice unto him, and said, What doest thou here, Elijah? And he said, I have been very jealous for the Lord God of hosts, because the children of Israel have forsaken thy covenant, thrown down thine altars, and slain thy prophets with the sword; and I, even I only, am left, and they seek my life, to take it away. And the Lord said unto him, Go, return on thy way to the wilderness of Damascus; and when thou comest, anoint Hazael to be king over Syria. And Jehu, the son of Nimshi, shalt thou anoint to be king over Israel. And Elisha, the son of Shaphat of Abel-meholah, shalt thou anoint to be prophet in thy stead. And it shall come to pass, that him that escapeth the sword of Hazael, shall Jehu slay; and him that escapeth from the sword of Jehu, shall Elisha slay. Yet I have left me seven thousand in Israel, all the knees which have not bowed unto Baal, and every mouth which hath not kissed him.

FROM A MOUNTAIN TO THE VALLEY

1 Kings 19:1–18

We have seen Elijah as the man of the hour on Mount Carmel — a mighty man of God who was brave, fearless and committed. We now come to an incident in Elijah's life that some of us would have omitted if we had written the Bible. One of the greatest evidences that the Bible is the Word of God and not the word of man is that it records not only the triumphs and victories of the men and women of God, but it also records their failures. The sin of David with Bathsheba, the sin of Moses by striking the rock twice instead of speaking to it, the sin of Abraham in lying about his wife, Sarah, and the despondency and the depression of Elijah — God's Word includes them all. If the Bible had a purely human origin, the authors would have omitted, or at least limited the weak points and failures of its characters, and exalted their good points. God's Word, however, includes for us the weaknesses as well as the strong points of the heroes of faith.

As we have beheld Elijah on the mountain victorious (1 Ki. 18), we now must view him in the valley defeated (1 Ki. 19). At this point the remarks of A. W. Pink are most appropriate: "In passing from 1 Kings 18 to 1 Kings 19 we meet with a sudden and strange transition. It is as though the sun was shining brilliantly out of a clear sky and the next moment, without any warning, black clouds drape the heavens and crashes of thunder shake the earth. The contrasts presented by these chapters are sharp and startling. At the close of the one 'the hand of the lord was on Elijah' as he ran before Ahab's chariot: at the beginning of the other he is occupied with self and 'went for his life.' In the former we behold the prophet at his best: in the latter we see him at his worst. There he was strong in faith and the helper of his people: here he is filled with fear and is the deserter of his nation. In the one he confronts the four hundred prophets of Baal undaunted: in the other he flees panic-stricken from the threats of one woman. From the mountain top he betakes himself into the wilderness, and from supplicating Jehovah that He would vindicate and glorify His great name to begging Him to take away his life. Who would have imagined such a tragic sequel?" Here, we are reminded vividly of the truth of James 5:17: "Elijah was a man subject to like passions as we are . . . ." In other words, Elijah was made of the *same stuff* as we are.

Elijah Despondent

"And Ahab told Jezebel all that Elijah had done, and how he had slain all the prophets with the sword. Then Jezebel sent a messenger unto Elijah, saying, So let the gods do to me, and more also, if I make not thy life as the life of one of them by tomorrow about this time. And when he saw that, he arose, and went for his life . . ." (1 Ki. 19:1–3).

How could it happen that a man who had been fearless and undaunted could then lose that courage and begin to run for his life? However, such an experience often happens with the child of God. A psychologist would call it despondency. Oftentimes, after a believer's greatest spiritual victories, he finds himself in what John Bunyan called the "Slough of Despond." A Christian should not be surprised if, after some great spiritual victory, a strange period of despondency arrives on the scene.

After this great spiritual experience on the mountaintop, Ahab told his wicked wife, Jezebel, what Elijah had done. She was the hand that ruled her weak-kneed husband. She wasn't impressed with the report, but replied, "I'm not afraid of him. In 24 hours, he's going to be dead" (paraphrased).

And then a strange thing transpired. This man of God, who was willing to stand up before the prophets of Baal, in the sight of the nation, turned one hundred eighty degrees and took off in the opposite direction.

Verse 3: "And when he saw that, he arose, and went for his life, and came to Beer-sheba, which belongeth to Judah, and left his servant there."

Beer-sheba is in the southern part of present-day Israel — 150 miles from Jezreel! There he left his servant, but he kept going.

Verse 4: "But he himself went a day's journey into the wilderness, and came and sat down under a juniper tree. And he requested for himself that he might die, and said, It is enough! Now, O Lord, take away my life; for I am not better than my fathers."

Why did he leave his servant there and keep

going? In simple terms, he was quitting the prophetic ministry. He was not planning on coming back to what he considered to be a land that was wicked beyond help. Then after another day's journey, he sat down under a juniper tree and asked God to take his life.

What in the world happened? Where is the Elijah of Mount Carmel? Where is the Elijah who stood before Ahab and pointed his finger toward him and said, "It's not going to rain for three years until I say so!" Are we reading about the same man?

Right after a great spiritual experience is the time when Satan's attacks are the strongest. When I was a pastor, it would happen like this. After a wonderful service of blessing at church, our family would pull out of the church parking lot, and about one-half mile down the road one of the kids would become sick in the car! What a way to deflate a spiritual bubble! There is a saying, "a pastor resigns from his church every Monday." That may not be true, but many pastors can identify with the feeling!

That's what happened to Elijah. He is on the mountaintop with God, and then a few hours later, after his great spiritual experience, he's leaving town and running from one woman. Simply stated, Elijah looked at circumstances and not at the Lord. When he first stood fearlessly before Ahab his eyes were on the Lord. At the lonely brook Cherith, his eyes were on the Lord. And then when he came down, he got his eyes on Jezebel. When we take our eyes off the Lord and look at the circumstances, we become candidates for despondency.

You recall that when Peter was walking on the

water, he had his eyes on the Lord, but when he saw the wind and the waves, what happened? Splash (Mt. 14:24–33)!

God used a tremendous therapy with Elijah. Verses 5–7: "And as he lay and slept under a juniper tree, behold, an angel touched him, and said unto him, Arise and eat. And he looked, and, behold, there was a cake baked on the coals, and a cruse of water at his head. And he did eat and drink, and laid down again. And the angel of the Lord came again the second time, and touched him, and said, Arise and eat, because the journey is too great for thee." Despondency or despair does not always come from spiritual or emotional causes. Oftentimes, it simply comes from physical causes — lack of sleep or poor eating habits. Satan often attacks us when we're tired. That was the first step in the Lord's therapeutic treatment of Elijah's despondency. Before He ever ministered to Elijah's spirit, He ministered to Elijah's body. There are some sincere Christian *workaholics* who boast "I would rather burn out than rust out." Such an attitude may sound very pious, but the truth of the matter is that *burning out* and *rusting out* are not the only two choices for the servant of the Lord to make. Such a choice sounds like the following: "Well, you're going to die so choose which way you want it — by the knife or by gun!"

There must be a balance where we can both abound in the work of the Lord (1 Cor. 15:58) and also come apart . . . and rest a while (Mk. 6:31). If we don't learn how to *come apart*, then we will soon do just that — *come apart!*

Elijah Depressed

"And he arose, and did eat and drink, and went in the strength of that food forty days and forty nights unto Horeb, the mount of God" (v. 8). He kept on going! He had gone 150 miles to Beer-sheba and then he kept on going to the southern part of the Sinai Peninsula where Horeb, which is another name for Mount Sinai, was located. This was 300 miles away from Jezreel and Jezebel. He came to Mount Sinai, the place where Moses, one of his illustrious predecessors, received the law from God; the place where Israel had made a covenant with God. Why would he go there? I believe he went there because he had given up on Israel. He wanted God to renew His covenant with him alone and start a new people, just as He had done with Moses 700 years before. In other words, what God had intended to do with Moses but didn't, Elijah now desires to be done with him (Ex. 32:9–14).

Verse 9: "And he came there unto a cave [the same *cave* where Moses was covered by God's hand in Ex. 33:22?], and lodged there; and, behold, the word of the Lord came to him . . . ." You'll notice how that is the first time in this passage that the word of God came to Elijah. In 1 Kings 17:2, 8 and 18:1, the Bible says "the word of the Lord came unto him," but in 19:3, it doesn't say that. Elijah was disobedient to God in running away from Jezebel. He was not following the word of the Lord as he had at previous times.

He's had some food, he's had some rest, so he can now think clearly. So God begins to deal with his spiritual problem.

Verse 9: ". . . What doest thou here, Elijah?" In other words, "Elijah, why are you here? You ought to be in Israel. The people there are perishing for lack of knowledge, and you're in the wrong place." Verse 10: ". . .I have been very jealous for the Lord God of hosts. For the children of Israel have forsaken thy covenant, thrown down thine altars, and slain thy prophets with the sword; and I, even I only, am left, and they seek my life, to take it away."

There is Elijah's depression. And now, he's in the grips of it because he's filled with self-pity. "I'm the only one left. And I've done a pretty good job, too. You've seen what I've done, Lord. I stood up to the prophets of Baal. I've stood up to Ahab" (paraphrased). Do you notice the number of I's? Elijah was a great man of God. Don't misunderstand me. My criticism of him is not because I have arrived, but because God had recorded it here for us to learn from it and appreciate it. This great man of God had taken his eyes off the Lord and started feeling sorry for himself. Have you ever felt sorry for yourself — a *pity party*, as it's called, and you're the only one invited? That's the mark of depression and despondency. "And I, even I only, am left." Elijah was in the real throes of depression, and he was useless to God. He was 300 miles away from the place that he ought to be, feeling sorry for himself. Elijah was despondent under a juniper tree; he was depressed in a cave; now notice that Elijah was delivered before the Lord.

Elijah Delivered

The Lord dealt with him in verses 11 and 12: "...
Go forth, and stand upon the mount before the
Lord. And, behold, the Lord passed by, and a great
and strong wind rent the mountains, and broke in
pieces the rocks before the Lord; but the Lord was
not in the wind. And after the wind an earthquake;
but the Lord was not in the earthquake. And after
the earthquake a fire; but the Lord was not in the
fire. And after the fire a still, small voice." Wind,
earthquakes, fire — all symbols of God's mighty
power, and Elijah had known that type of ministry.
He had been the one who had thundered, who had
blown, who had quaked. He had been a man of
power, but somehow, God was teaching him a
lesson here. God was not in any of these things, but
He was very present in a "still, small voice."

What was He teaching Elijah by showing him
these noisy manifestations of nature followed by a
quiet word? Great natural catastrophes like those
mentioned can quickly destroy men's lives, but
only the "still, small voice" of the Holy Spirit can
regenerate men through the patient teaching of the
Word. Elijah's problem was shared by the two
disciples of Jesus who wanted a Samaritan village,
which had refused them hospitality, to be destroy-
ed by fire from Heaven — Elijah style! They were
rebuked by the Savior for their wrong spirit (Lk.
9:55). In the same way, God does not always work in
such outward displays of vengeance. Elijah's new
type of ministry was to be of the "still, small voice"
variety, in contrast to the preceding dramatic

measures.

Verses 13 and 14: "And it was so, when Elijah heard it, that he wrapped his face in his mantle, and went out, and stood in the entrance of the cave. And, behold, there came a voice unto him, and said, What doest thou here, Elijah? And he said, I have been very jealous for the Lord God of hosts, because the children of Israel have forsaken thy covenant, thrown down thine altars, and slain thy prophets with the sword; and I, even I only, am left, and they seek my life, to take it away." Now God begins to deal with His depressed prophet. Verse 18: "Yet I have left me seven thousand in Israel, all the knees which have not bowed unto Baal, and every mouth which hath not kissed him." With that answer, He dealt with Elijah's excuse — "I'm the only one left." In effect, God said to His prophet: "You are not indispensable, Elijah, you're not the only one. And if you go and do something else and forsake the prophetic ministry, I may just get one of those 7,000 to do it. Don't think that you're a privileged character with God." Don't think that because you suppose you are the only one doing the work, that you have some sort of special privilege.

Dear reader, don't think that you're indispensable to God. You may be in the throes of despondency and despair simply because you are convinced that you have to carry the whole weight of some responsibility.

Now, how does God deal with the depression of Elijah? Verses 15–17: "And the Lord said unto him, Go, return on thy way to the wilderness of Damascus; and when thou comest, anoint Hazael to be king over Syria. And Jehu, the son of Nimshi, shalt thou anoint to be king over Israel. And Elisha, the son of Shaphat of Abelmeholah, shalt thou anoint to be prophet in thy stead. And it shall come to pass, that him that escapeth the sword of Hazael, shall Jehu slay; and him that escapeth from the sword of Jehu, shall Elisha slay." He told Elijah to do three things: Anoint a king of Syria, anoint Jehu as king of Israel, and anoint Elisha as his (Elijah's) successor. One of the greatest problems with depressed people is that they have lost their willingness to serve the Lord. They are sitting around doing nothing, feeling sorry for themselves. One of the best therapies is simply to get busy. The cure for Elijah's depression was to get his eyes on the Lord, to recognize that he was not indispensable, and then to get busy and stop feeling sorry for himself. Get your focus outward and not inward. Get your eyes off yourself and get them on the Lord. Get your eyes off the problems and on the tasks at hand. Get busy for the Lord and stop feeling sorry for yourself. That's the best therapy you can have. Elijah did that, and thank God, because of his tremendous deliverance at the hand of the Lord, his ministry was not over. Because he was delivered from this abominable depression, much of his greatest ministry still lay ahead. True, it was a different type of ministry. Gone were the days of Mount Carmel, but Elijah was not to be *put on the shelf*. The inspired admonition of the apostle will serve well to close this chapter of Elijah's life. "And let us not be weary in well doing; for in due season we shall reap, if we faint not" (Gal. 6:9).

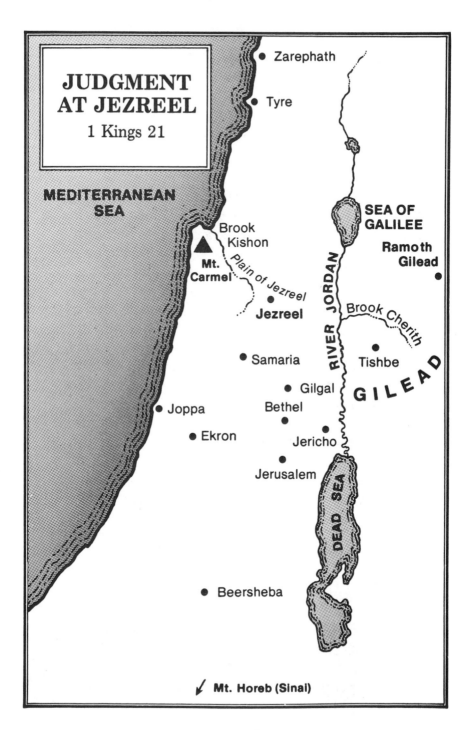

JUDGMENT
AT JEZREEL
1 Kings 21

MEDITERRANEAN
SEA

Zarephath

Tyre

Brook
Kishon

Mt.
Carmel

Plain of Jezreel

Jezreel

SEA OF
GALILEE

Ramoth
Gilead

RIVER JORDAN

Brook Cherith

Samaria

Tishbe

Gilgal

GILEAD

Bethel

Joppa

Ekron

Jericho

Jerusalem

DEAD SEA

Beersheba

Mt. Horeb (Sinai)

7

1 Kings 21

And it came to pass after these things, that
Naboth, the Jezreelite, had a vineyard, which was in
Jezreel, close to the palace of Ahab, king of Samaria.
And Ahab spoke unto Naboth, saying, Give me thy
vineyard, that I may have it for a garden of herbs,
because it is near unto my house, and I will give thee
for it a better vineyard than it; or, if it seem good to
thee, I will give thee the worth of it in money. And
Naboth said to Ahab, The Lord forbid me, that I
should give the inheritance of my fathers unto thee.
And Ahab came into his house sullen and displeased
because of the word which Naboth, the Jezreelite,
had spoken to him; for he had said, I will not give thee
the inheritance of my fathers. And he lay down upon
his bed, and turned away his face, and would eat no
food. But Jezebel, his wife, came to him, and said
unto him, Why is thy spirit so sad, that thou eatest no
food? And he said unto her, Because I spoke unto
Naboth, the Jezreelite, and said unto him, Give me
thy vineyard for money; or else, if it please thee, I will
give thee another vineyard for it; and he answered, I
will not give thee my vineyard. And Jezebel, his wife,
said unto him, Dost thou now govern the kingdom of
Israel? Arise, and eat food, and let thine heart be
merry. I will give thee the vineyard of Naboth, the
Jezreelite. So she wrote letters in Ahab's name, and
sealed them with his seal, and sent the letters unto the

elders and to the nobles who were in his city, dwelling with Naboth. And she wrote in the letters, saying, Proclaim a fast, and set Naboth on high among the people. And set two men, worthless fellows, before him, to bear witness against him, saying, Thou didst blaspheme God and the king. And then carry him out, and stone him, that he may die. And the men of his city, even the elders and the nobles who were the inhabitants in his city, did as Jezebel had sent unto them, and as it was written in the letters which she had sent unto them. They proclaimed a fast, and set Naboth on high among the people. And there came in two men, worthless fellows, and sat before him; and the worthless men witnessed against him, even against Naboth, in the presence of the people, saying, Naboth did blaspheme God and the king. Then they carried him forth out of the city, and stoned him with stones, so that he died. Then they sent to Jezebel, saying, Naboth is stoned, and is dead. And it came to pass, when Jezebel heard that Naboth was stoned, and was dead, that Jezebel said to Ahab, Arise, take possession of the vineyard of Naboth, the Jezreelite, which he refused to give thee for money; for Naboth is not alive, but dead. And it came to pass, when Ahab heard that Naboth was dead, that Ahab rose up to go down to the vineyard of Naboth, the Jezreelite, to take possession of it. And the word of the Lord came to Elijah, the Tishbite, saying, Arise, go down to meet Ahab, king of Israel, who is in Samaria; behold, he is in the vineyard of Naboth, where he is gone down to possess it. And thou shalt speak unto him, saying, Thus saith the Lord, Has thou killed, and also taken possession? And thou shalt speak unto him, saying, Thus saith the Lord, In the place where dogs licked the blood of Naboth, shall dogs lick thy blood, even thine. And Ahab said to Elijah, Hast thou found me, O mine enemy? And he answered, I have found thee, because thou hast sold thyself to work evil in the sight of the Lord. Behold, I will bring evil upon thee, and will take away thy posterity, and will cut off from Ahab every male, and him who is shut up and left in Israel; And will make thine house like the house of Jeroboam, the son of Nebat, and like the house of Baasha, the son of Ahijah, for the provocation with which thou hast provoked me to anger, and made Israel to sin. And of Jezebel also spoke the Lord, saying, The dogs shall eat Jezebel by the wall of Jezreel. Him that dieth of Ahab in the city, the dogs shall eat; and him that dieth in the field, shall the fowls of the air eat. But there was none like unto Ahab, who did sell himself to work wickedness in the sight of the Lord, whom Jezebel, his wife, stirred up. And he did very abominably in following idols, according to all things as did the Amorites, whom the Lord cast out before the children of Israel. And it came to pass, when Ahab heard those words, that he tore his clothes, and put sackcloth upon his flesh, and fasted, and lay in sackcloth, and went softly. And the word of the Lord came to Elijah, the Tishbite, saying, Seest thou how Ahab humbleth himself before me? Because he humbleth himself before me, I will not bring the evil in his days; but in his son's days will I bring the evil upon his house.

JUDGMENT IN JEZREEL

1 Kings 21

In the land of Israel a broad valley stretches thirty-six miles from the port city of Haifa on Mount Carmel southeastward to the Jordan River. This fertile plain separates the mountains of Galilee to the north from those of Samaria to the south. This fertile expanse has been given many names over the years: the Valley of Esdraelon, the Valley of Jezreel, and in the New Testament, *Armageddon*. It has been the scene of numerous military encounters through the centuries. It was on this soggy expanse that the armies of Barak routed those of Sisera (Jud. 4). It was here that Gideon routed the Midianites with his band of 300 (Jud. 7). It was here that Saul visited the woman of Endor and then died with his son Jonathan at the hands of the Philistines (1 Sam. 28, 31). It was here that King Josiah met his death at the hands of Pharaoh-neco (2 Ki. 23:29). It was here that Allenby routed the Turks during the First World War in 1917, and here the fledgling Israeli army defeated an Iraqi contingent in 1948. It shall be here also that the armies of the world will marshal their forces to prepare to fight "the battle of that great day of God Almighty" (Rev. 16:14).

The bleak ruins of the little town of Jezreel rest quietly today on the southern edge of that valley. If they could speak, those silent sentinels of stone would relate many absorbing tales which they have witnessed over the centuries. Not the least of those accounts would be the one that lies before the reader of 1 Kings 21. It was in Jezreel that the wicked King Ahab had built a magnificent palace to rival the one his father, Omri, had built in Samaria twenty miles to the south. It was to Jezreel that Ahab fled following the disastrous defeat of his Baal prophets on Mount Carmel (1 Ki. 18:45–46), and it was from this winter palace that he ruled with his domineering and evil wife, Jezebel. It was here also that a simple Israelite citizen named Naboth had the unfortunate lot of owning a vineyard next to Ahab's palace. It was at Jezreel that Ahab met for the final time his old nemesis, Elijah. Finally, it was in Jezreel where Jezebel experienced the awful judgment of Almighty God. A king, a farmer, a queen, and a prophet were the actors in a tragic drama which one writer has aptly titled, *Payday Someday*.

The King and the Farmer

During this period of apostasy when only a few thousand Israelites were not bowing the knee to Baal (1 Ki. 19:18), it is encouraging to read about the spiritual commitment of a man like Naboth. Naboth owned a plot of ground that he had inherited from his father and that had been kept in the family for many generations. He was faithful in tending and cultivating a beautiful vineyard that had been planted on that land. It was not his fault that Ahab's palace happened to adjoin his property.

We can imagine that one day Ahab was overlooking the area from his balcony when he noticed his next-door neighbor busily at work in his vineyard. Ahab did not need another vineyard (he owned plenty of them), but how nice it would be, he thought, if he had a fertile plot of land close by on which he could cultivate some special herbs with which to season his royal meals.

Ahab approached his neighbor with what looks like a very fair offer: ". . . Give me thy vineyard, that I may have it for a garden of herbs, because it is near unto my house, and I will give thee for it a better vineyard than it; or, if it seem good to thee, I will give thee the worth of it in money" (v. 2). The offer was simple: Naboth could trade his vineyard to Ahab for a better one located elsewhere, or Ahab would pay him a fair price to purchase it outright.

Some modern readers may be surprised at Naboth's response: "And Naboth said to Ahab, The Lord forbid me, that I should give the inheritance of my fathers unto thee" (v. 3). Was Naboth trying to hold out for a better offer? Was he trying to upstage the powerful king and make him come begging for the deal? Or was he simply a stubborn old miser standing his ground in the face of modern change? None of these possibilities can adequately explain Naboth's refusal to close the transaction. Naboth's firmness was based on his commitment to the Word of God. Before the Israelites ever settled in the Promised Land, God commanded that they should never sell a paternal inheritance (Lev. 25:23; Num. 36:7). The land was to be kept in the family. Thus, God's Word forbade Naboth from selling the land, and he was ready to stand up to anyone, even the king, to obey that command. Such *spiritual stubbornness* is greatly needed in our day of lukewarm compromise when principle is often sacrificed for expediency. One might try to argue that with this offer Naboth could secure for himself and his family a better and more productive vineyard provided by Ahab! But situation ethics was as wrong in Naboth's day as it is today. ". . . Behold, to obey is better than sacrifice, and to hearken than the fat of rams" (1 Sam. 15:22).

Ahab had every right to make Naboth an offer, but his reaction to Naboth's refusal graphically reveals his childish immaturity: "And Ahab came into his house sullen and displeased because of the word which Naboth, the Jezreelite, had spoken to him; for he had said, I will not give thee the inheritance of my fathers. And he lay down upon his bed, and turned away his face, and would eat no food" (v. 4). Big, bad Ahab! The sight of a monarch with lower lip protruding, stomping into his bedroom and flinging himself upon his bed, facing the wall and refusing to eat is enough to make us laugh if it were not so sad.

The King and the Queen

"But Jezebel, his wife, came to him, and said unto him, Why is thy spirit so sad, that thou eatest no food?" (v. 5). Ahab was a weak man, and there is no sadder spectacle than a weak man domineered by a strong woman. The whole matter would have ended had not Jezebel entered the picture. What has been said of this woman up to this point has revealed her to be a cunning instrument of Satan to turn away the hearts of God's people from the truth. In one of those politically expedient marriages between royal houses, Ahab had taken Jezebel as his wife, "And it came to pass, as if it had been a light thing for him to walk in the sins of Jeroboam, the son of Nebat, that he took as his wife Jezebel, the daughter of Ethbaal, king of the Sidonians, and went and served Baal, and worshiped him" (1 Ki. 16:31). This evil princess had arrived at the royal palace accompanied by her patron deity, Baal. Soon she had succeeded in introducing the worship of this foreign nature god into large areas of the kingdom. Her campaign of paganization was accompanied by an outright persecution of the true prophets of God (1 Ki. 18:4, 13). It was Jezebel who buckled Elijah's knees with her threat to his life following the defeat of her Baal prophets on Carmel (1 Ki. 19:1–2). Truly this woman was a personification of evil in its worst form. When the Lord Jesus accused the church of Thyatira of spiritual fornication, He called the instigator of the affair by the name of this wicked woman (Rev. 2:20–23). Probably no female name is associated with such insidious cruelty as Jezebel. Ahab would probably have forgotten the whole "Naboth affair," but the next events reveal graphically the truth of 1 Kings 21:25: "But there was none like unto Ahab, who did sell himself to work wickedness in the sight of the Lord, *whom Jezebel, his wife, stirred up.*"

When she discovered the reason for Ahab's sadness, the poison of her malevolent personality was poured out in a diabolical plan. A woman like Jezebel was not at all concerned whether her husband had an herb garden or not — it was the principle of *autocratic executive power* that was at stake. The rights of the individual (i.e., Naboth) must always take second place to the dictatorial whims of an absolute monarch.

In the midst of all her wickedness, Jezebel manifested a sort of evil brilliance. Her plan to secure Naboth's vineyard for Ahab had all the trappings of piety and legality. An official letter from the king with his own seal was to be sent to the officials of the city. It should be noted that her first sin was *forgery*, for she would write the letters herself and employ Ahab's seal (v. 8). Her second sin was *hypocrisy*, for she called for a fast to be proclaimed (v. 9). This fast was to call attention to the fact that some great sin had been committed that caused God's displeasure against the city. Evil people will often use religion to serve their evil ends. Her third sin was *perjury*, for the letters called for two "sons of Belial" (i.e., *scoundrels*) to give a false testimony implicating the innocent Naboth (v. 10). Their charge was that Naboth had cursed God and the king — a capital offense under the law (Lev. 24:14). Sadly, there are always people who can be found to whom truth is a valueless commodity, especially when they can sell it for a high price (cf. Mt. 26:59–62). The fourth sin committed by Jezebel and company that day was *murder*: ". . . Then they carried him forth out of the city, and stoned him with stones, so that he died" (v. 13). A later reference informs us that Naboth's sons, his rightful heirs to the property at his death, also shared the same fate as their condemned father (2 Ki. 9:26). A grieving widow and mother was heard weeping in Jezreel that night, bereft of those closest to her. A man had simply chosen to follow God rather than man, and his life had been snuffed out by a scheming queen and a weak king who had acquiesced to her malevolent plan.

When the news of the travesty of justice reached the royal couple, Ahab arose to take official possession of the vineyard. The whole incident was covered with a veneer of *legality*. If a man died leaving no heirs, his property reverted to the care of the state. Now the head of that state entered the vineyard to secure it for himself.

The King and the Prophet

At this point in the sordid affair, one might ask, *Will this crime be allowed to take place? Is there no justice? Where is God?* To all appearances, Naboth's disinheritance and murder was the *perfect crime*. The citizens of Jezreel were no doubt convinced that their unfortunate neighbor deserved his fate. Only a very few were privy to the dastardly plot concocted by Jezebel. The stage was now set for Ahab to enjoy his *prize* without fear of interference by anyone.

However, Ahab and Jezebel had ignored the truth expressed by an earlier king of Israel in Proverbs 15:3, "The eyes of the Lord are in every place, beholding the evil and the good." Jehovah God had not allowed the wicked deed to go unnoticed. It was now time for Him to act. He revealed His word to Elijah, informing the prophet of Ahab's deed and instructing him to deliver a message of judgment to the king (vv. 17–19).

Ahab entered the vineyard and was basking in

his new acquisition, when he was rudely awakened by the figure of a man clothed in camel hair with eyes ablaze with the fire of God. Ahab vividly remembered this wild looking character. It was he who had announced the drought of three years on the land (1 Ki. 17:1). It was he who had engineered the defeat of Jezebel's *darling* prophets on Mount Carmel (1 Ki. 18:19–40).

"And Ahab said to Elijah, Hast thou found me, O mine enemy? And he answered, I have found thee, because thou hast sold thyself to work evil in the sight of the Lord" (v. 20). Without delay, Elijah continued to deliver one of the most stunning declarations of judgment in the Word of God. Elijah prophesied the following: (1) Every male child of Ahab's will die (v. 21); (2) Ahab's dynasty will cease, just as Jeroboam's and Baasha's came to an untimely end (v.22); (3) Jezebel will be eaten by dogs in Jezreel (v. 23); and (4) dogs will lick up the blood of Ahab, as they had done to Naboth (vv. 19, 24).

The message of judgment fell on Ahab like a crushing stone: "And it came to pass, when Ahab heard those words, that he tore his clothes, and put sackcloth upon his flesh, and fasted, and lay in sackcloth, and went softly" (v. 27). He did not argue with Elijah. The prophet had been proven right too many times before. The immediate effect on the king was that he put on all the trappings of outward repentance — the rending of garments, the sackcloth, the fasting. It is also added that "he went softly," or "walked about slowly," like one in deep trouble. A great Bible scholar remarks on this passage, "This repentance was neither hypocritical, nor purely external; but it was sincere even if it was not lasting and produced no real conversion" (C. F. Keil). The Lord himself acknowledged it to be a real repentance, "Seest thou how Ahab humbleth himself before me? Because he humbleth himself before me, I will not bring the evil in his days; but in his son's days will I bring the evil upon his house" (v. 29). The judgment was not revoked, it was simply postponed. The calamity upon Ahab's house did not take place in his lifetime, but in the days of his son, Joram. This was later graphically fulfilled in the murder of Joram by Jehu and the casting of his corpse in the stolen plot of ground in Jezreel (2 Ki. 9:24–26), followed immediately by the execution of the remaining seventy sons of Ahab (2 Ki. 10:1–11).

Once more, Elijah displayed great courage in delivering this message of judgment. It was an unpopular message, but sorely needed and most appropriate. The message of God's wrath is even more unpopular today. False views of God's love are spread abroad in our day, but the fact remains that before a sinner can understand the love of God, he must first understand the holiness of God. Elijah's message that God is angry with the wicked needs to be thundered out again in this ungodly age in which we live.

The King and God

The Bible does not state how long Ahab continued to *go softly* and display evidence of his repentance. Evidently, Elijah departed as suddenly as he had appeared. As three years passed (1 Ki. 22:1), the memory of this dramatic encounter began to fade from Ahab's mind. His kingdom continued to prosper outwardly. Perhaps Ahab concluded that this time Elijah had been wrong in his prediction of judgment. A war with Syria, however, provided the context in which God's judgment would take place.

Along with Jehoshaphat, king of Judah, Ahab rode off to Gilead beyond Jordan to recover the captured town of Ramoth. Even though another prophet named Micaiah had prophesied his demise (1 Ki. 22:17), Ahab rode off confidently, deceived by an evil spirit (vv. 19–24). In the heat of the conflict, "... a certain man drew a bow at a venture [lit. *at random*], and smote the king of Israel between the joints of his armor ..." (v. 34). When that Syrian archer released his arrow, he had no idea that the God of Heaven would reach down and guide its flight directly to a vulnerable spot in Ahab's armor. Such is the method that God often uses to accomplish His purposes. The king was severely wounded, and even though he tried to stay in the battle, he eventually died. Ahab was buried in Samaria: "And one washed the chariot in the pool of Samaria, and the dogs licked up his blood; and they washed his armor, according unto the word of the Lord which he spoke" (v. 38). How appropriate the poetic justice of God! How faithful the word of judgment spoken three years earlier by the prophet! Ahab could not escape the righteous judgment of God though the passage of time seemed to indicate otherwise.

But what about Jezebel, the evil hand that ruled Ahab and the mind that hatched the plan that murdered poor Naboth? Fifteen years passed slowly, and Jezebel continued unscathed and safe. Even though she retired from public life, no great catastrophe of judgment had fallen on her as Elijah had announced. The poet, Longfellow, graphically captured in verse the solemn truth played out on the pages of Scripture:

> Though the mills of God grind slowly,
>   Yet they grind exceeding small;
> Though with patience He stands waiting,
>   With exactness grinds He all.

Another king from another family had ascended the throne of Israel by force. After bloodily smiting Joram, the son of Ahab, Jehu rode to Jezreel to execute his wrath on Jezebel. The eunuchs who lived in the palace with her were only too willing to throw her out the window at the feet of Jehu's horses. The account in 2 Kings 9:33–36 is most graphic: "And he said, Throw her down. So they threw her down. And some of her blood was sprinkled on the wall, and on the horses; and he trod her under foot . . . And they went to bury her; but they found no more of her than the skull, and the feet, and the palms of her hands. Wherefore they came again, and told him. And he said, This is the word of the Lord, which he spoke by his servant, Elijah the Tishbite, saying, In the portion of Jezreel shall dogs eat the flesh of Jezebel" (vv. 33, 35, 36).

The perfect crime was not so perfect after all! Ahab and Jezebel had not reckoned on the omniscient Jehovah God and His righteousness. Yes, there will be a *Payday Someday* for everyone who has flaunted the Word of God thinking he can get away unnoticed and unpunished. The psalmist wondered how God could allow the wicked to prosper, "Until I went into the sanctuary of God; then understood I their end. Surely, thou didst set them in slippery places; thou castedst them down into destruction" (Ps. 73:17–18). "For they have sown the wind, and they shall reap the whirlwind ..." (Hos. 8:7). The apostle expressed it this way: "Be not deceived, God is not mocked, for whatever a man soweth, that shall he also reap" (Gal. 6:7).

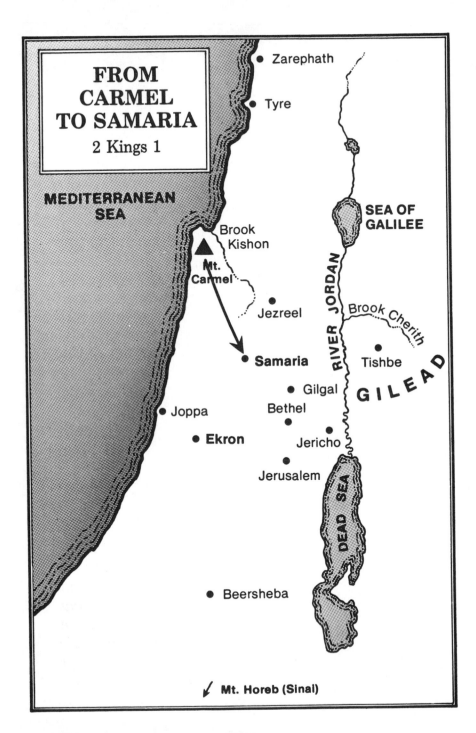

FROM
CARMEL
TO SAMARIA
2 Kings 1

MEDITERRANEAN
SEA

Zarephath

Tyre

SEA OF
GALILEE

Brook
Kishon

Mt.
Carmel

Jezreel

Brook Cherith

RIVER JORDAN

Samaria

Tishbe

Gilgal

GILEAD

Joppa

Bethel

Ekron

Jericho

Jerusalem

DEAD SEA

Beersheba

↙ Mt. Horeb (Sinai)

8

2 Kings 1:1–17a

Then Moab rebelled against Israel after the death of Ahab. And Ahaziah fell down through a lattice in his upper chamber that was in Samaria, and was sick. And he sent messengers, and said unto them, Go, inquire of Baal-zebub, the god of Ekron, whether I shall recover from this disease. But the angel of the Lord said to Elijah, the Tishbite, Arise, go up to meet the messengers of the king of Samaria, and say unto them, Is it because there is not a God in Israel, that ye go to inquire of Baal-zebub, the god of Ekron? Now, therefore, thus saith the Lord, Thou shalt not come down from that bed to which thou art gone, but shalt surely die. And Elijah departed. And when the messengers returned unto him, he said unto them, Why are ye now returned? And they said unto him, There came a man up to meet us, and said unto us, Go, return unto the king who sent you, and say unto him, Thus saith the Lord, Is it because there is not a God in Israel, that thou sendest to inquire of Baal-zebub, the god of Ekron? Therefore, thou shalt not come down from that bed to which thou art gone, but shalt surely die. And he said unto them, What manner of man was he who came up to meet you, and told you these words? And they answered him, He was an hairy man, and girded with a belt of leather around his waist. And he said, It is Elijah, the Tishbite. Then the king sent unto him a captain of fifty with his fifty. And he went up to him, and, behold, he sat on the top of an hill. And he spoke unto him, Thou man of God, the king hath said, Come down. And Elijah answered and said to the captain of fifty, If I be a man of God, then let fire come down from heaven, and consume thee and thy fifty. And there came down fire from heaven, and consumed him and his fifty. Again also he sent unto him another captain of fifty with his fifty. And he answered and said unto him, O man of God, thus hath the king said, Come down quickly. And Elijah answered and said unto them, If I be a man of God, let fire come down from heaven, and consume thee and thy fifty. And the fire of God came down from heaven, and consumed him and his fifty. And he sent again a captain of the third fifty with his fifty. And the third captain of fifty went up, and came and fell on his knees before Elijah, and besought him, and said unto him, O man of God, I pray thee, let my life, and the life of these fifty, thy servants, be precious in thy sight. Behold, there came fire down from heaven, and burned up the two captains of the former fifties with their fifties; therefore, let my life now be precious in thy sight. And the angel of the Lord said unto Elijah, Go down with him; be not afraid of him. And he arose, and went down with him unto the king. And he said unto him, Thus saith the Lord, Forasmuch as thou hast sent messengers to inquire of Baal-zebub, the god of Ekron, is it because there is no God in Israel to inquire of his word? Therefore, thou shalt not come off that bed to which thou art gone, but shalt surely die. So he died according to the word of the Lord which Elijah had spoken.

ELIJAH AND AHAZIAH

2 Kings 1:1–17a

Whenever a citizenry groans under the burden of an incompetent political leader, they always can take hope that someday there will be a change. In a democracy, that change can come at election time. In a monarchy, however, the death of the ruler provides the only opportunity for *relief*. In ancient Israel the rule of Ahab certainly was a burden to his subjects. He had married a pagan foreign princess, Jezebel (1 Ki. 16:31). He had sponsored the open worship of the false god Baal (1 Ki. 16:32–33). During his reign the disastrous three and a half year drought had plagued the land (1 Ki. 18:1). Furthermore, he had led the nation's army into a disastrous military campaign against the Syrians (1 Ki. 22). With his death in that battle, there was no doubt anticipation of a *better day* coming. That *day* was not to be, however, for his son and successor, Ahaziah, proved to be his equal in evil.

Moab's Move

"Then Moab rebelled against Israel after the death of Ahab" (2 Ki. 1:1). Moab was one of Israel's neighbors on the eastern side of the Dead Sea. They traced their ancestry to one of the sons of Lot

(Gen. 19:37). The Moabites had been enemies of Israel for many years. Balak, King of Moab, had sought to thwart the Israelites in their journey to the Promised Land by hiring Balaam to curse them (Num. 22–24). Moab was not completely subdued by Israel until the military campaigns of King David, "And he [David] smote Moab, and measured them with a line, casting them down to the ground; even with two lines measured he to put to death, and with one full line to keep alive. And so the Moabites became David's servants, and brought gifts" (2 Sam. 8:2). For over 200 years the Moabites had been paying tribute to the kings of Israel. "And Mesha, king of Moab, was a sheep breeder, and rendered unto the king of Israel an hundred thousand lambs, and an hundred thousand rams, with the wool" (2 Ki. 3:4). Having been oppressed by the wicked kings Omri and Ahab, they seized an opportunity for rebellion after Ahab's death. The complete story of this rebellion, led by Mesha, king of Moab, is recounted in 2 Kings 3:5–27. Its relevance to this account is to point up the continuing unsettled nature of the community to which Elijah was called to minister. God had promised many times that if His people would follow Him wholly, He would cause defeat of their enemies. "And it shall come to pass, if thou shalt hearken diligently unto the voice of the Lord thy God, to observe and to do all his commandments which I command thee this day, that the Lord thy God will set thee on high above all nations of the earth," "The Lord shall cause thine enemies who rise up against thee to be smitten before thy face; they shall come out against thee one way, and flee before thee seven ways" (Dt. 28:1, 7). Conversely, if they departed from the Lord, they could expect defeat at the hands of their enemies. "But it shall come to pass, if thou wilt not hearken unto the voice of the Lord thy God, to observe to do all his commandments and his statutes which I command thee this day, that all these curses shall come upon thee, and overtake thee," "The Lord shall cause thee to be smitten before thine enemies; thou shalt go out one way against them, and flee seven ways before them, and shalt be removed into all the kingdoms of the earth" (Dt. 28:15, 25).

An interesting confirmation of this event was unearthed in 1868. A German missionary named Klein discovered a stone monument at Dibon in the ancient land of Moab (modern-day "Jordan"). On the monument was an inscription of thirty-four lines written by Mesha, King of Moab, to commemorate his revolt against Israel mentioned in 2 Kings 1 and 3. Both Omri and Ahab are mentioned in the inscription as being oppressors of Moab.

For the believer in the Bible such confirmation from archaeology is not needed. To the skeptic, however, this and many other discoveries have served to confirm that the Bible is true in whatever it says.

Ahaziah's Accident

"And Ahaziah fell down through a lattice in his upper chamber that was in Samaria, and was sick. And he sent messengers, and said unto them, Go, inquire of Baal-zebub, the god of Ekron, whether I shall recover from this disease" (2 Ki. 1:2). The wicked King Ahab had ruled Israel for approximately 20 years (822–802 B.C.) His son Ahaziah's rule was for only two years (802–800 B.C.). A capsule summary of his character is given in the previous chapter. "And he [Ahaziah] did evil in the sight of the Lord, and walked in the way of his father, and in the way of his mother, and in the way of Jeroboam, the son of Nebat, who made Israel to sin; For he served Baal, and worshiped him, and provoked to anger the Lord God of Israel, according to all that his father had done" (1 Ki. 22:52–53). Like father, like son! If there were ever any hope for an improvement on Ahab, that hope was dashed during the brief reign of that wicked king's son. The only other reference to Ahaziah is his ill-fated ship-building venture with Jehoshaphat of Judah. "And after this did Jehoshaphat, king of Judah, join himself with Ahaziah, king of Israel, who did very wickedly. And he joined himself with him to make ships to go to Tarshish; and they made the ships in Ezion-geber. Then Eliezer, the son of Dodavahu of Mareshah, prophesied against Jehoshaphat, saying, Because thou hast joined thyself with Ahaziah, the Lord hath broken thy works. And the ships were broken, that they were not able to go to Tarshish" (2 Chr. 20:35–37).

One day Ahaziah was relaxing in the upper chamber of his palace in Samaria. Evidently he leaned against the "lattice," a protective screen over the window, and it gave way, causing him to fall through the window. We do not know the extent of his injuries and the resulting "disease" (fever?), but they must have been severe enough to make him wonder if he would recover. Had he been a follower of Jehovah, this would have provided an excellent opportunity to seek out a "man of God," express his repentance, and seek the Lord's favor. Ahaziah, however, only wanted to know, "Will I recover?" and he sought this answer from "Baal-zebub, the god of Ekron," not from the Lord.

"Baal" means "lord" or "master." In modern Hebrew it is actually the word for "husband." When the Israelites entered the land of Canaan they encountered many Canaanite deities, each of which was a "master" or "owner" of a section of land. The gods of individual localities had appropriate surnames, e.g. Baal-peor (Num. 25:3). The name referred generally to the storm and fertility god of the Canaanites in its many manifestations. Elijah's ministry directed itself against Baal in all his forms. Elijah reminded Ahab, "I have not troubled Israel; but thou, and thy father's house, in that ye have forsaken the commandments of the Lord, and thou hast followed Baalim [plural of Baal]" (1 Ki. 18:18). The false god which Ahaziah sought to inquire of was Baal-zebub, which means literally, "Lord of the Flies." This was the local deity whose shrine was at Ekron, one of the Philistine cities (Josh. 13:2–3). As far as can be discerned, the fly was worshiped in some way at Ekron. The reference, however, may be to the deity that supposedly could protect from the flies. Whatever be the actual nature of this false deity, later Jews deliberately corrupted its pronunciation to Baal-zebul, meaning "Lord of the Dunghill." It is in this form that it appears in the Greek original of Matthew 12:24, where it is referred to as the "prince of the demons." In any case, Ahaziah seeks the advice of this nonexistent deity much as the ancient Greeks would seek advice from the famous oracle of Delphi. In this the king of Israel proved himself no higher than the pagans in his conception of the deity.

Elijah's Eloquence

"But the angel of the Lord said to Elijah, the Tishbite, Arise, go up to meet the messengers of the king of Samaria, and say unto them, Is it because there is not a God in Israel, that ye go to inquire of Baal-zebub, the god of Ekron? Now, therefore, thus saith the Lord, Thou shalt not come down from that bed to which thou art gone, but shalt surely die. And Elijah departed" (2 Ki. 1:3–4). The "angel of the Lord" was a visible manifestation of the Lord himself He appeared to Abraham (Gen. 18) to Jacob (Gen. 32), to Moses (Ex. 3), and to many others in the Old Testament. A study of the passages reveals that the "angel of the Lord" was actually a preincarnate appearance of Jesus Christ. The message of the Lord which Elijah was to deliver was a stern rebuke and promise — because of his seeking Baal-zebub and not Jehovah, Ahaziah would never recover but would die in his bed! "Since he is so anxious to know his fate, this is it, let him make the best of it." The Hebrew construction reads literally, "dying, thou shalt die."

It is the exact same promise given by God to Adam in Genesis 2:17: "But of the tree of the knowledge of good and evil, thou shalt not eat of it; for in the day that thou eatest thereof thou shalt surely die." Other appearances of this dour prediction are Exodus 19:12, Numbers 26:65, 1 Kings 2:37, and Ezekiel 3:18.

After Elijah had intercepted Ahaziah's messengers and delivered this ominous announcement, they returned to Ahaziah and told him of it (vv. 5–6). When they described to the king that the announcer of his doom was a "hairy man, and girded with a belt of leather about his waist," he knew it was "Elijah, the Tishbite" (v. 8). Evidently a coarse garment was characteristic of a prophet. Even a false prophet would appear this way (Zech. 13:4)! The coarseness of their clothing stood out as a rebuke to the luxurious life style that they often rebuked. When John the Baptizer appeared with his message of repentance he is described this way, "And the same John had his raiment of camel's hair, and a leather belt about his waist; and his food was locusts and wild honey" (Mt. 3:4). He that was clothed with the Spirit despised all rich and gay clothing.

This was evidently the first and only contact that Ahaziah was to have with the mighty prophet. If he dreamed that Elijah had tormented only his father, he had a rude awakening on his sick bed. Matthew Henry stated eloquently, "He that was a thorn in Ahab's eyes will be so in the eyes of his son while he treads in the steps of his father's wickedness."

Jehovah's Judgment

Ahaziah was faced with a choice. On the one hand, he could accept the prophet's message, acknowledge his sinful ways, and plead for God's mercy. This was what happened with his father Ahab when Elijah delivered much the same message to him, "And it came to pass, when Ahab heard those words, that he tore his clothes, and put sackcloth upon his flesh, and fasted, and lay in sackcloth, and went softly" (1 Ki. 21:27). Although his outward "repentance" did not avert God's judgment, it did postpone it. "Seest thou how Ahab humbleth himself before me? Because he humbleth himself before me, I will not bring the evil in his days; but in his son's days will I bring the evil upon his house" (1 Ki. 21:29). His father's example, however, was lost on his son. On the other hand, he could have repudiated Elijah's message as the rantings of a wild fanatic and carried through his idolatrous plan. Elijah had been proven right too many times, however. Therefore, Ahaziah thought he might bargain with the prophet. He sent a group of fifty soldiers with their captain with the message to "Come down" (v. 9). They found Elijah on the "top of an hill," possibly Mount Carmel, which may have been Elijah's abode (cf. 1 Ki. 18:42). Elijah was not interested in bargaining with the king. His answer to Ahaziah's demand was, "And Elijah answered and said to the captain of fifty, If I be a man of God, then let fire come down from heaven, and consume thee and thy fifty. And there came down fire from heaven, and consumed him and his fifty" (v. 10). The king had the audacity to send another fifty with the added demand, "Come down **quickly**" (v. 11). This group met the same fate as the first (v.12). The callous Ahaziah then had the audacity to send a third embassage. The captain of this group, however, had learned from the experience of his former colleagues and pleaded for the lives of his company (vv. 13, 14). It was then that the "angel of the Lord" assured Elijah that it was safe to go with this group to the king (v. 15). This last verse gives us the answer to the problem of the morality of this passage. Some have wondered why Elijah would call down fire on soldiers who were simply obeying orders and were not personally guilty. Evidently, however, the first two companies had more than an escort planned for Elijah. His life would have been in danger had he gone with them. No soldier is responsible to obey orders if those orders are from a wicked and perverse king who orders the destruction of righteous people. Their judgment was just.

Elijah, therefore, made his last "royal appearance." He wasted no time in bargaining, however. He delivered the announcement of Jehovah's judgment, "Thus saith the Lord, Forasmuch as thou hast sent messengers to inquire of Baal-zebub, the god of Ekron, is it because there is no God in Israel to inquire of his word? Therefore, thou shalt not come down off that bed to which thou art gone, but shalt surely die" (v. 16). "So he died according to the word of the Lord which Elijah had spoken" (v. 17a).

Elijah's **public** ministry thus came to a close in the same way it began — with the announcement of judgment to a wicked king (cf. 1 Ki. 17:1).

Disciples' Desire

This dramatic incident was cited by two of Jesus' disciples in an interesting incident recorded only by Luke. "And it came to pass, when the time was come that he should be received up, he steadfastly set his face to go to Jerusalem, And sent messengers before his face; and they went, and entered into a village of the Samaritans, to make ready for him. And they did not receive him, because his face was as though he would go to Jerusalem. And when his disciples, James and John, saw this, they said, Lord, wilt thou that we command fire to come down from heaven, and consume them, even as Elijah did? But he turned and rebuked them, and said, Ye know not what manner of spirit ye are of; For the Son of man is not come to destroy men's lives, but to save them. And they went to another village" (Lk. 9:51–56).

The conclusion of Jesus' *Galilean* ministry had arrived. It was now time to turn His direction toward Jerusalem, the city where He would be rejected and suffer (Lk. 9:22). Instead of taking the circuitous route around Samaria, as most Jews did in His day, Jesus decided to walk directly south through Samaria as He had done earlier in His ministry (Jn. 4:1–42). He sent messengers ahead to make lodging preparations. One of the Samaritan villages, however, refused to receive Jesus' party. The reason was "because his [Jesus'] face was as though he would go to Jerusalem" (v. 53). The Samaritans were descendents of pagans who had been brought to this area by the Assyrian king over seven hundred years earlier (2 Ki. 17:24–41). They intermarried with some of the surviving Jews and developed their own *homemade* religion, acknowledging only the first five books of Moses as authoritative. They even established a rival temple to Jerusalem's on Mount Gerizim (cf. Jn. 4:20). Therefore, when these Samaritans realized that Jesus was actually heading for Jerusalem's Temple, they refused to show Him any hospitality at all.

This rebuff prompted the following suggestion by some of Jesus' disciples: "And when his disciples, James and John, saw this, they said, Lord, wilt thou that we command fire to come down from heaven, and consume them, even as Elijah did?" (Lk. 9:54). James and John were brothers, the sons of Zebedee. Evidently, when Jesus called them to His service, He recognized their volatile nature because He gave them the surname "Boanerges, which is, **The sons of thunder**" (Mk. 3:17).

Here this thunderous pair desired to emulate Elijah's deed and thunder judgment from Heaven on these rude Samaritans. Jesus, however, would allow no such treatment. He rebuked them and reminded them that the purpose of His coming was to save men's lives, not to destroy them (vv. 55–56). It is important to note what Jesus was **not** doing and what He **was** doing. Jesus was not approving of the Samaritan worship, nor was He disapproving of Elijah's action recorded in 2 Kings 1. Jesus was stating that the principles on which His kingdom was based were spiritual and not physical. The way to conquer men's hearts is not by the sword of destruction, but by the sword of the Spirit. It would have been good if succeeding generations of Christ's Church had heeded this rebuke given by Christ. Tens of thousands have been put to death for religion's sake in the annals of church history by those who thought they were God's appointed Elijahs! The Apostle Paul later remarked, "For the weapons of our warfare are not carnal, but mighty through God to the pulling down of strongholds" (2 Cor. 10:4). The days of the Old Testament *theocracy* are over. The spiritual nature of Christ's kingdom demands spiritual methods. It is instructive to note that the Apostle John, at a later period when he had grown in grace, came down to Samaria in a very different spirit. He came with Peter not to call fire down from Heaven, but to confer spiritual blessings on the Samaritans. And we are told that he "preached the gospel in many villages of the Samaritans" (Acts 8:25). The excellent thought of one of the classic commentators on the life of Elijah, F. W. Krummacher, should serve to apply this incident to our lives. "It therefore infinitely more becomes us as followers of the Lamb, to pray for the enemies of His righteous cause, than to desire God's displeasure upon them. It is unspeakably more befitting us, in patience and meekness to heap coals of fire on the heads of our adversaries, and to overcome them by the power of love; than to call down the wrath of the Almighty upon them. In short, our whole disposition and conduct ought to evidence that we are the disciples of Him who 'came not to destroy men's lives, but to save them;' and that, by the cross of Christ, a fountain of love has been disclosed, which has taught us to bear all things, to believe all things, and endure all things; a love which many waters cannot quench."

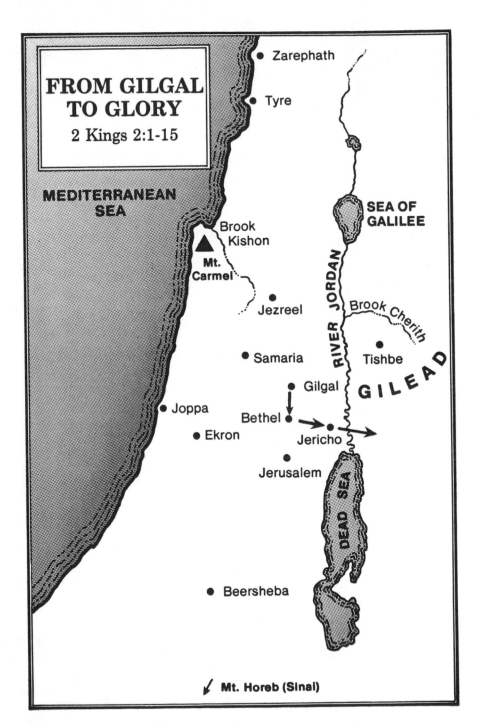

FROM GILGAL
TO GLORY
2 Kings 2:1-15

MEDITERRANEAN
SEA

Zarephath

Tyre

Brook
Kishon

Mt.
Carmel

Jezreel

SEA OF
GALILEE

RIVER JORDAN

Brook Cherith

Samaria

Tishbe

GILEAD

Gilgal

Bethel

Joppa

Jericho

Ekron

Jerusalem

DEAD SEA

Beersheba

Mt. Horeb (Sinai)

9

2 Kings 2:1–15

And it came to pass, when the Lord would take up Elijah into heaven by a whirlwind, that Elijah went with Elisha from Gilgal. And Elijah said unto Elisha, Tarry here, I pray thee; for the Lord hath sent me to Bethel. And Elisha said unto him, As the Lord liveth, and as thy soul liveth, I will not leave thee. So they went down to Bethel. And the sons of the prophets who were at Bethel came forth to Elisha, and said unto him, Knowest thou that the Lord will take away thy master from thy head today? And he said, Yea, I know it; hold ye your peace. And Elijah said unto him, Elisha, tarry here, I pray thee; for the Lord hath sent me to Jericho. And he said, As the Lord liveth, and as thy soul liveth, I will not leave thee. So they came to Jericho. And the sons of the prophets who were at Jericho came to Elisha, and said unto him, Knowest thou that the Lord will take away thy master from thy head today? And he answered, Yea, I know it; hold your peace. And Elijah said unto him, Tarry, I pray thee, here; for the Lord hath sent me to the Jordan. And he said, As the Lord liveth, and as thy soul liveth, I will not leave thee. And they two went on. And fifty men of the sons of the prophets went, and stood to view afar off; and they two stood by the Jordan. And Elijah took his mantle, and wrapped it together, and smote the waters, and they were divided to the one side and to the other, so that they two went over on dry ground. And it came to pass, when they were gone over, that Elijah said unto Elisha, Ask what I shall do for thee, before I am taken away from thee. And Elisha said, I pray thee, let a double portion of thy spirit be upon me. And he said, Thou hast asked a hard thing. Nevertheless, if thou see me when I am taken from thee, it shall be so unto thee; but if not, it shall not be so. And it came to pass, as they still went on, and talked, that, behold, there appeared a chariot of fire, and horses of fire, and separated them, and Elijah went up by a whirlwind into heaven. And Elisha saw it, and he cried, My father, my father, the chariot of Israel, and its horsemen. And he saw him no more; and he took hold of his own clothes, and tore them in two pieces. He took up also the mantle of Elijah that fell from him, and went back, and stood by the bank of the Jordan. And he took the mantle of Elijah that fell from him, and smote the waters, and said, Where is the Lord God of Elijah? And when he also had smitten the waters, they parted to the one side and to the other; and Elisha went over. And when the sons of the prophets, who were looking on at Jericho, saw him, they said, The spirit of Elijah doth rest on Elisha. And they came to meet him, and bowed themselves to the ground before him.

ELIJAH'S CORONATION DAY

2 Kings 2:1–15

The coronation of an earthly monarch usually takes place early in life and commences his reign. For the believer, however, his coronation day takes place at death when he is raised to a higher realm of glory. Such is the case with Elijah who would never have been mistaken for a king during his earthly life. Yet, when his task on earth was over, God elevated him to His throne in Heaven by a supernatural exit from this world.

We do not know exactly how Elijah spent his last days, but he probably gave much of his time to teaching "the sons of the prophets" (1Ki. 20:35; 2 Ki. 2:3, 5, 7, 15; 4:1, 38). These were groups of young men who had begun to exercise their prophetic gift under the tutelage of a more experienced "man of God." Such work, though not as spectacular as the performing of miracles, was of even greater importance in the ongoing work of God. The time spent by Christ in training the apostles produced more lasting fruit than the miracles He performed before the multitudes. In training others, Elijah insured that his ministry would *multiply* rather than simply *add* results. This model of ministry is urged upon New Testament pastor-teachers in Ephesians 4:11–12: "And he gave some, apostles; and some, prophets; and some, evangelists; and some, pastors and teachers; For the perfecting of the saints for the work of the ministry for the edifying of the body of Christ." It was while he was engaged in this last great work of his life that God called him home.

The Test

"And it came to pass, when the Lord would take up Elijah into heaven by a whirlwind, that Elijah went with Elisha from Gilgal. And Elijah said unto Elisha, Tarry here, I pray thee; for the Lord hath sent me to Bethel. And Elisha said unto him, As the Lord liveth, and as thy soul liveth, I will not leave thee. So they went down to Bethel" (2:1–2). We can rest assured that God had revealed to Elijah that his *day* had arrived. While he was with his successor Elisha at Gilgal, Elijah asked him to remain behind while he departed. Elisha steadfastly refused. This request was simply to test the strength of Elisha's commitment and faith. Elisha had said earlier, "I will follow thee" (1 Ki. 19:20). But would he cleave to the prophet to the end? His tenacity reminds us of Ruth's decision to follow Naomi even after she had been discouraged from doing so: "And Ruth said, Entreat me not to leave thee, or to turn away from following after thee; for where thou goest, I will go; and where thou lodgest, I will lodge: thy people shall be my people, and thy God, my God" (Ruth 1:16).

When the pair made their next stop at Bethel, the sons of the prophets joined in by stating that to follow Elijah was fruitless because the Lord was taking him that day. But Elisha remained firm in his resolve to accompany his mentor (2:3–4).

Finally, they arrived at Jericho, near the banks of the Jordan River. There, another group of fledgling prophets repeated the discouraging refrain. Elijah also again urged Elisha to remain on this side of the river while he departed. But the spiritually resolute Elisha was not to be deterred (2:5–6).

Elisha's determination not to *look back* is an example to all who desire the full blessing of the Lord on their ministries. "And Jesus said unto him, No man, having put his hand to the plough, and looking back, is fit for the kingdom of God" (Lk. 9:62). It was Jacob's determination to continue wrestling with God that resulted in his being blessed: "... I will not let thee go, except thou bless me" (Gen. 32:26).

In many ways Elisha and Elijah were different. While Elijah grew up in the poor area of Gilead, Elisha probably came from a wealthy family (1 Ki. 19:19). While Elijah preferred the rural outdoors, Elisha was more at home in cities and palaces. While Elijah seemed to be a man of extreme moods, Elisha appeared more even-tempered. One characteristic, however, they shared in common — a godly inflexibility that insured their success against the ungodly forces of their day.

Even though the curious "sons of the prophets" desired to witness Elijah's translation (2:7), only Elisha was permitted to see the event. "And Elijah took his mantle, and wrapped it together, and smote the waters, and they were divided to the one side and to the other, so that they two went over on dry ground" (2:8). That mantle was the badge of

Elijah's distinctive office (cf. 1 Ki. 19:13, 19). It was with his rod that Moses had divided the sea (Ex. 14:16); here it was with his mantle that Elijah divided the river. The classic commentator, Matthew Henry, long ago remarked on this incident: "The miraculous dividing of the river Jordan was the preface of Elijah's translation into heavenly Canaan, as it had been to the entrance of Israel into the earthly Canaan. He and Elisha might have gone over Jordan by a ferry, but God would magnify Elijah in his exit, as he did Joshua in his entrance."

This parting of the Jordan was the last miracle with which Elijah was associated. The others were: (1) the drought (1 Ki. 17:1); (2) the sustenance at Brook Cherith (1 Ki. 17:2–6); (3) the sustenance of the widow's house (1 Ki. 17:8–16); (4) the raising of the widow's son (1 Ki. 17:17–24); (5) the fire from Heaven on Carmel (1 Ki. 18:21—39); (6) the prayer for rain (1 Ki. 18:41—46); (7) the destruction of Ahaziah's soldiers (2 Ki. 1:2–12).

The Request

"And it came to pass, when they were gone over, that Elijah said unto Elisha, Ask what I shall do for thee, before I am taken away from thee. And Elisha said, I pray thee, let a double portion of thy spirit be upon me" (2:9).

Elijah offered to Elisha anything that his heart desired! He could do this because he knew that his young successor would not abuse such a privilege. Years before the Lord appeared to the young Solomon and said, "Ask what I shall give thee." He could do this because He knew that Solomon would not request long life, riches, or a military victory, but an understanding heart (1 Ki. 3:5–12). This is the thinking behind Psalm 37:4: "Delight thyself also in the Lord, and he shall give thee the desires of thine heart." We cannot claim the last part of that verse unless we fulfill the first part. If we truly place the Lord first in our hearts, then the desires of our hearts will be in accordance with His will.

The request for a "double portion" of Elijah's spirit may appear perplexing, but understanding the usage of this Old Testament phrase will help us to understand its meaning here. The law declared that the firstborn son had the right to inherit a "double portion" of his father's estate. "But he shall acknowledge the son of the hated for the first-born, by giving him a double portion of all that he hath; for he is the beginning of his strength; the right of the firstborn is his" (Dt. 21:17). In legal terminology, this is called the right of *primogeniture*. Elisha did not ask for something superior to that which his master enjoyed, but for a portion "double" that which was communicated to the other prophets. Elisha looked upon himself as the firstborn son of Elijah in relation to the other "sons of the prophets." One might see a parallel here to the statement by the Lord Jesus in John 14:12, "Verily, verily, I say unto you, He that believeth on me, the works that I do shall he do also; and greater works than these shall he do, because I go unto my father," particularly when this promise of the Lord was associated also with the coming of the Spirit (Jn. 14:16ff.).

Elijah acknowledged the hardness of his request, but promised the answer if Elisha never removed his eyes from him until he was gone (2:10). The big moment finally arrived, "And it came to pass, as they still went on, and talked, that, behold, there appeared a chariot of fire, and horses of fire, and separated them, and Elijah went up by a whirlwind into heaven" (2:11). Their pleasant journey was interrupted when a fiery chariot pulled by fiery horses came between them. This would not be the last time that Elisha would experience such a visitation from a heavenly entourage. In 2 Kings 6:17, the Lord opened the eyes of Elisha's fearful servant so he could see the "horses and chariots of fire round about Elisha." From this parallel passage and Psalm 68:17 ("The chariots of God are twenty thousand, even thousands of angels . . ."), it is safe to conclude that the chariot and horses were mighty angels sent to conduct Elijah to Heaven (cf. Lk. 16:22: "And it came to pass that the beggar died, and was carried by the angels into Abraham's bosom; the rich man also died, and was buried"). The popular artist's conception of Elijah as riding *in* the chariot is not stated in the text. The chariot actually came *between* the two prophets while "Elijah went up by a whirlwind into heaven" (2:11).

"And Elisha saw it, and he cried, My father, my father, the chariot of Israel, and its horsemen. And he saw him no more; and he took hold of his own clothes, and tore them in two pieces" (2:12). Elisha followed his master's orders right to the end. Yet even though he knew that the prophet would be taken, his grief at the departure was still great. The rending of garments was a sign of mourning among the Hebrews (Gen. 37:29; 44:13; 2 Sam. 3:31; Joel 2:13). It should be noted that Elisha called Elijah

". . . the chariot of Israel, and its horsemen . . ."
(2:12). The significance of this title can be understood by noting that when Elisha later was dying, King Joash lamented his condition by addressing him with the same title (see 2 Ki. 13:14). Ancient kings measured their strength by the number of horses and chariots they possessed. This phrase is a reminder that the greatness of Israel lay not in armaments, but in spiritual men of God who were the real strength of the nation. Although Elisha bewailed the loss of this true pillar of strength, he replaced that pillar himself.

The Bequest

"He took up also the mantle of Elijah that fell from him, and went back, and stood by the bank of the Jordan" (2:13). At the funeral of a great Christian leader whom many thought could never be replaced, a speaker reminded the sad hearers, "God buries His workmen, but He carries on His work!" Elijah was gone, but his mantle fell to the ground to be worn now by another prophet of God.

"And he took the mantle of Elijah that fell from him, and smote the waters, and said, Where is the Lord God of Elijah? And when he also had smitten the waters, they parted to the one side and to the other; and Elisha went over. And when the sons of the prophets, who were looking on at Jericho, saw him, they said, The spirit of Elijah doth rest on Elisha. And they came to meet him, and bowed themselves to the ground before him" (2:14–15). Elijah's last miracle was Elisha's first miracle. He had learned well. His cry, "Where is the Lord God of Elijah?" reminds us that even though Elijah was missing, Elijah's God was still present and active in the continuing ministry of his successor.

Elisha commenced a ministry that was destined to bring help to the needy (2 Ki. 4:1–7); joy to the bereaved (2 Ki. 4:18–37); health to the sick (2 Ki. 5:1–14); judgment to the wicked (2 Ki. 6:8–23); and life to the dead (2 Ki. 13:20–21). Although to compare Elijah and Elisha would be unfair to both, it is interesting that Elisha's ministry lasted about twice as long as Elijah's and that he apparently performed twice as many miracles as his illustrious predecessor. This is further evidence of the "double portion" of Elijah's spirit resting on his successor.

Elijah, however, was privileged to have a part in two events which Elisha and no other prophet ever experienced. First, Elijah passed through the portals of Heaven without dying. Enoch, "the seventh from Adam" (Jude 14), was the only other person privileged to pass directly from earth to Heaven without experiencing death: "And Enoch walked with God, and he was not; for God took him" (Gen. 5:24). How privileged, therefore, are those saints who are alive at the time of the coming of the Lord Jesus! "Behold, I show you a mystery: We shall not all sleep, but we shall all be changed, In a moment, in the twinkling of an eye, at the last trump; for the trumpet shall sound, and the dead shall be raised incorruptible, and we shall be changed" (1 Cor. 15:51–52). The songwriter has graphically described that "rapture" mentioned also by Paul in 1 Thessalonians 4:16–17 and experienced personally by Elijah. "Oh joy! Oh delight! should we go without dying, No sickness, no sadness, no dread and no crying, Caught up thru the clouds with our Lord into glory, When Jesus receives 'His own.' " Secondly, Elijah was chosen to play a role in prophecy, i.e., to return to this earth again. "Behold, I will send you Elijah, the prophet, before the coming of the great and terrible day of the Lord" (Mal. 4:5). The fulfillment of that remarkable prophecy will be explained in the last chapter, "Elijah's Future."

Thus ended the earthly existence of one of the greatest men of God who ever lived. He labored in a remote corner of this earth. He had not much of this world's goods. He had none of the world's applause. No city council ever elected him "man of the year." When he left, there were evidently no memorial services for him, no monuments erected in his memory, or no parks named in his honor. But the Lord God afforded him the greatest privilege imaginable — a heavenly escort to bring him bodily to glory without having to taste of death. He sought in his life to please God alone — it was God alone who rewarded him!

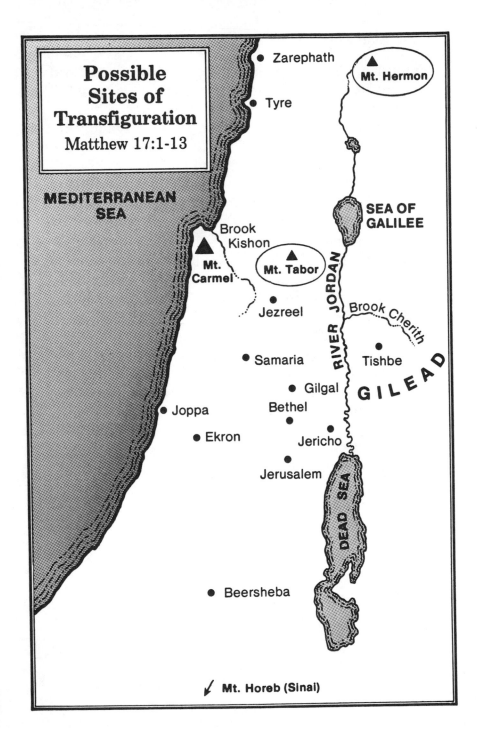

Possible
Sites of
Transfiguration
Matthew 17:1-13

MEDITERRANEAN
SEA

Zarephath

Mt. Hermon

Tyre

SEA OF
GALILEE

Brook
Kishon

Mt. Tabor

Mt.
Carmel

Jezreel

RIVER JORDAN

Brook Cherith

Samaria

Tishbe

GILEAD

Gilgal

Joppa

Bethel

Ekron

Jericho

Jerusalem

DEAD SEA

Beersheba

Mt. Horeb (Sinai)

10
Malachi 4:5–6

Behold, I will send you Elijah, the prophet, before the coming of the great and terrible day of the Lord; And he shall turn the heart of the fathers to the children, and the heart of the children to their fathers, lest I come and smite the earth with a curse.

Matthew 17:1–13

And after six days Jesus taketh Peter, James, and John, his brother, and bringeth them up into an high mountain privately, And was transfigured before them; and his face did shine like the sun, and his raiment was as white as the light. And, behold, there appeared unto them Moses and Elijah talking with him. Then answered Peter, and said unto Jesus, Lord, it is good for us to be here; if thou wilt, let us make here three booths; one for thee, and one for Moses, and one for Elijah. While he yet spoke, behold, a bright cloud overshadowed them; and, behold, a voice out of the cloud, which said, This is my beloved Son, in whom I am well pleased; hear ye him. And when the disciples heard it, they fell on their face, and were very much afraid. And Jesus came and touched them, and said, Arise, and be not afraid. And when they had lifted up their eyes, they saw no man, except Jesus only. And as they came down from the mountain, Jesus charged them, saying, Tell the vision to no man, until the Son of man is raised again from the dead. And his disciples asked him, saying, Why then say the scribes that Elijah must first come? And Jesus answered and said unto them, Elijah truly shall first come, and restore all things. But I say unto you, That Elijah is come already, and they knew him not, but have done unto him whatsoever they desired. Likewise shall also the Son of man suffer of them. Then the disciples understood that he spoke unto them of John the Baptist.

ELIJAH'S FUTURE
Malachi 4:5–6; Matthew 17:1–13

Elijah's supernatural departure from this earth (2 Ki. 2:9–11) was certainly a unique privilege afforded to the great prophet. Only one other, Enoch the seventh from Adam (Jude 14), has been exempted from walking "through the valley of the shadow of death" (Ps. 23:4; Gen. 5:24). Since Elijah did not die one might except that he could return again someday to his place of ministry. That is exactly what a later prophet taught. As a matter of fact, the last word in the Old Testament is a prophecy concerning this great man of God. "Behold, I will send you Elijah, the prophet, before the coming of the great and terrible day of the Lord; And he shall turn the heart of the fathers to the children, and the heart of the children to their fathers, lest I come and smite the earth with a curse" (Mal. 4:5–6). It is the purpose of this chapter to explore how that prophecy was developed in the New Testament and in later Jewish tradition.

Elijah,
John The Baptist, And Jesus

The appearance of John the *Baptizer* (literal translation) in Judea prior to Jesus' public ministry must have caused many to compare him to the Prophet Elijah. John came out of the wilderness, as Elijah did (Lk. 1:80; 1 Ki. 17:1). John wore a hairy garment with a leather belt as Elijah did (Mt. 3:4; 2 Ki. 1:8). John issued a strong message of repentance and judgment, as Elijah did (Mt. 3:7–12; 1 Ki. 17:1; 18:21).

When the angel announced to Zacharias the birth of John, he described the child in this way: "And he shall go before him in the spirit and power of Elijah . . ." (Lk. 1:17a). It is not surprising, therefore, that the priests and Levites from Jerusalem asked John, "Art thou Elijah?" John unequivocally answered, "I am not" (Jn. 1:21). It is important to note John's clear denial that he was Elijah because some teach that Malachi's prophecy found its complete fulfillment in John. By John's own word, this is simply not so. But this does not mean that John had no prophetic relationship to Elijah. A consideration of the account of the transfiguration and its aftermath will help to answer the question.

Matthew 17:1–9 records that Jesus took the inner circle of His disciples, Peter, James, and John, into a high mountain. The location of this event is disputed, but many believe it took place on one of the ridges of the majestic Mount Hermon in northern Galilee. Others hold to the traditional site of Mount Tabor at the eastern end of the Jezreel Valley. While they were there the disciples received a preview of the glorious return of Christ as He was *transfigured* (Greek: *metamorphosed*) before them. Suddenly, two other figures appeared at the Lord's side . . . Moses and Elijah, the great representatives of the law and the prophets. Luke informs us that they discussed with Jesus his approaching death in Jerusalem (Lk. 9:31). Interest in the Messiah's death was something that constantly fascinated the Old Testament saints (cf. 1 Pet. 1:10–11). Without thinking, Peter suggested that three tabernacles or booths be built on the very spot. During the Feast of Tabernacles the people of Israel were to construct temporary booths (tabernacles) in which they would live for a week (cf. Lev. 23:33– 43). Most probably Peter thought that the Kingdom had arrived since the Feast of Tabernacles will be observed during that blessed period (Zech. 14:16). This was not to be the case, however. The Father corrected Peter's shortsightedness by reminding him that His Son was the One to be heeded. As great as Moses and Elijah were, they could not be placed on the same level with His Son. Jesus then commanded them not to report the vision until He had risen from the dead.

As the disciples descended the mountain their minds were racing with thoughts and questions. Isn't Elijah supposed to come **before** the day of the Lord and the Kingdom? Didn't we just see Elijah? Why isn't the Kingdom about to arrive? Finally they burst out, ". . . Why then say the scribes that Elijah must first come? And Jesus answered and said unto them, Elijah truly shall first come, and restore all things. But I say unto you, That Elijah is come already, and they knew him not, but have done unto him whatsoever they desired. Likewise shall also the Son of man suffer of them. Then the disciples understood that he spoke unto them of John the Baptist" (Mt. 17:10–13). It is important to note that Jesus affirmed the scribal interpretation: "Elijah truly shall first come ..." (v. 11). Even after the transfiguration appearance, the Lord still spoke of Elijah's coming as yet future. John the Baptist did not fulfill **all** of the conditions involved in the prophecy of Malachi 4:5–6. However, in the person and ministry of John, Elijah had come in a certain sense. As John came in the **power** of Elijah before Messiah's first coming, so Elijah will come in **person** before Messiah's second coming. Since there would be two comings of the Messiah, the first time to suffer and the second time to reign, so also there must be two forerunners. Jesus then makes the point that just as John suffered, so would He. In other words, a suffering forerunner was to be followed by a suffering Messiah. Malachi's prophecy, therefore, was not completely fulfilled in John the Baptist. Yet no one doubted that John did come "in the spirit and power of Elijah."

Elijah In Jewish Tradition

There is a wealth of material on Elijah in rabbinical literature. The spirit of this character fired the imaginations of ancient and medieval rabbis who spun out hundreds of tales depicting the prophet's appearances and exploits after his supernatural departure from earth. Furthermore, there is a wealth of material on Elijah in Muslim tradition. Because of space, however, we must limit ourselves to what the rabbis said about Elijah's role after his departure to Heaven.

There are two types of material in rabbinic literature. The first is called *halacha (rule)*, which is legal material on what the law of God is and how to obey it. The second is called *haggadah (narration)* and is sermonic material consisting of parables, stories, legends and maxims. This material is not always considered as historically true, but was viewed as helping the Jewish people to better appreciate the character of these great spiritual heroes. The haggadah contains abundant references to Elijah. Since there is more about Elijah than about any other biblical character, only a summary of the facts about him can be given.

There is much in Jewish tradition about Elijah's relation to the Messiah. For example, Elijah is presently comforting the Messiah in His long wait for His time to come. It must be remembered that Judaism does not teach that Jesus is the Messiah, but that the Messiah has not yet come. When the time of final redemption arrives, Elijah will, according to one tradition, appear to call Israel to repentance and to announce that the Messiah is about to appear — evidently because he is well-known to the people while Messiah is unknown. Jewish tradition actually teaches that there will be two future messiahs — Messiah ben Joseph who will suffer and die in battle with the forces of Gog and Magog; and Messiah ben David who will conquer the wicked armies and reign in the Kingdom period. During the forty-five day period between the comings of these two *messiahs*, Elijah will read aloud the legendary Book of Jasher referred to in Joshua 10:13 and 2 Samuel 1:18–27. This reading will be sufficient enough to make the earth swallow the enemies of Israel.

When Elijah comes he will supposedly settle all

143

disputes, questions, and interpretations of the law. Furthermore, he will perform a series of miracles, one of which is to reveal the hiding place of the *lost ark*! (Wouldn't that make a great movie?) Finally, Elijah will take the shofar and give a tremendous blast which will cause the dead to rise.

Elijah also was supposed to have appeared personally to many of the great Jewish rabbis and mystics. In these appearances he instructed them, answered their questions, and comforted them in their poverty and suffering. Rabbi Simeon ben Yohai, the reputed author of the *Zohar* (the Jewish classic of mysticism), is said to have been instructed in the mysteries of Kabbalah during the thirteen years that he was hiding from the Romans in a cave. One interesting custom in modern Jewish observance is associated with Elijah. When an eight day old Jewish boy is circumcised in a ceremony called the *bris*, the chair in which the grandfather sits holding the baby is called the chair of Elijah. This custom goes back to the story of the circumcision of Rabbi Isaac Luria in the sixteenth century. When the ceremony was delayed, Elijah appeared to his father and held the child. Afterward he said to the father "Take good care of him, for he will spread a brilliant light throughout the world."

The personality of Elijah remains in the forefront of the Jewish mind through the ritual of the *havdala*, which marks the end of the Sabbath. Songs are sung recalling Elijah's deeds with one refrain stating, "the prophet Elijah, the Tishbite from Gilead, may he come to us soon with the son of David, the Messiah."

The most striking of all rituals connected with

Elijah occurs during the Passover Seder. A cup of wine is reserved on the table for him and at a fixed moment in the proceedings a door is opened for Elijah while a child is dismissed to see if the great prophet has arrived to join the family. What a privilege it would be for him to join the family for it would mean that the Messiah would be "close on his heels."

But does Elijah come? Perhaps it would be best to answer that question with a Hasidic story of a pious Jew who asked his rabbi: "For forty years I have opened the door for Elijah waiting for him to come, but he never does. What is the reason?" The rabbi answered: "In your neighborhood there lives a very poor family. Call the father and propose that you celebrate the next Passover in his house and that you will provide his family with everything necessary for the Passover season. Then on the Seder night Elijah will come." The man did as the rabbi told him, but later he claimed that again he had waited in vain to see Elijah. The rabbi answered: "I know very well that Elijah came on the Seder night to the house of your poor neighbor, but you could not see him." The rabbi then held a mirror before the man's face and said, "Look, this was Elijah's face that night."

Elijah And The Last Days

The ministry of Elijah had been one of calling apostate Israel back to the Lord whom they had forsaken. According to Malachi 4:5–6 he will come again in order to avert the curse of God from Israel. This work John the Baptist did not fully accomplish in his ministry. Is there any indication in the New Testament that Elijah will personally return?

In the Book of The Revelation there is a fascinating passage that may answer that question. Revelation 11:3–13 describes the three and one-half year ministry of two *witnesses*. This period corresponds to the first half of Daniel's *seventieth week*, i.e. the seven-year period preceding the revelation of Christ to inaugurate the Millennial Kingdom. This period precedes "the time of Jacob's trouble" (Jer. 30:7), a period of unparalleled suffering also called the "great tribulation" (Mt. 24:21; Rev. 7:14), answering to the **last** half of the seven-year period. When these two witnesses conclude their testimony, they are killed by the beast (i.e., the Antichrist), and their bodies are then mocked in the streets of Jerusalem, but they are finally raised up by God to Heaven. The result of the entire spectacle is that "the remnant were terrified, and gave glory to the God of heaven" (Rev. 11:13).

While the identity of these two is not given in the chapter, the miracles they perform are strikingly similar to the great Old Testament personalities, Moses and Elijah. It is interesting also that it was these two Old Testament heroes who appeared with Jesus at the transfiguration (Mt. 17:3–4). Two of their miracles (fire devouring their enemies and being able to shut off the rain) recall miracles of Elijah (cf. 2 Ki. 1:10–12; 1 Ki. 17:1). The other two miracles (turning water to blood and smiting the earth with plagues) recall Moses' ministry in Egypt (Ex. 7–10). A problem with this suggested identity is that Moses has already died once. Some, therefore, have identified the two as Enoch and Elijah, inasmuch as they did not die but were translated. There is agreement, however, that **one** of the witnesses is Elijah.

Therefore, the appearance of Elijah in Revelation 11:3–13 would be the final fulfillment of the prophecy in Malachi 4:5–6. How thankful we should be that we have the completed revelation of the New Testament, so we were not left to speculate about Elijah's activities, as was so often the case with medieval Jewish tradition.

The impact of Elijah the Tishbite was overwhelming, extending far beyond his ministry in the ninth century B.C. to the distant future. Truly he was one of the greatest men who ever lived. But our perspective should not be lost as we admire this man of God. Returning to the account of the transfiguration, we are reminded of One who is greater than all the heroes of Israel. After Moses and Elijah appeared with Jesus and talked with Him, and while Peter was making his rash suggestion, God the Father gave the final word on the matter: "While he [Peter] yet spoke, behold, a bright cloud overshadowed them; and, behold, a voice out of the cloud, which said, This is my beloved Son, in whom I am well pleased; hear ye him. And when the disciples heard it, they fell on their face, and were very much afraid. And Jesus came and touched them, and said, Arise, and be not afraid. And when they had lifted up their eyes, *they saw no man, except Jesus only*" (Mt. 17:5–8).

Truly One greater than Elijah has come! It is important, therefore, that we fix our gaze on Jesus. We can learn much from the great heroes of faith, but it is the Messiah who is the central theme of

Scripture. And it is He who is to have "pre-eminence" (Col. 1:18) — both in creation and in the hearts of His followers.

TRULY ONE GREATER THAN ELIJAH HAS COME!